ENCOUNTERS

Encounters

My life with Nixon, Marcuse,
and Other Friends and Teachers

Paul Gottfried

WILMINGTON, DELAWARE

Copyright © 2009 Paul Gottfried

All rights reserved. No part of this publication may be reproduced or transmitted in any form or by any means, electronic or mechanical, including photocopy, or any information storage and retrieval system now known or to be invented, without permission in writing from the publisher, except by a reviewer who wishes to quote brief passages in connection with a review written for inclusion in a magazine, newspaper, or broadcast.

Gottfried, Paul.

    Encounters: my life with Nixon, Marcuse, and other friends and teachers / Paul Gottfried. — 1st ed.— Wilmington, Del.: ISI Books, c2009.

    p. ; cm.
    ISBN: 978-1-933859-99-6
    Includes bibliographical references and index.

    1. Gottfried, Paul. 2. Conservatism—United States—History—20th century. 3. United States—Politics and government—1945–1989.
I. Title.

E743 .G664 2009   2008938527
320.52/0973—dc22   0905

    ISI Books
    Intercollegiate Studies Institute
    3901 Centerville Road
    Wilmington, DE 19807-0431
    www.isibooks.org

    Manufactured in the United States of America

Contents

Introduction		VII
I	*Apam*	1
II	A Life Recalled	19
III	The Marcuse Factor	45
IV	A Religious Visionary	63
V	A Flamboyant Friend	77
VI	Three Central Europeans	97
VII	Two Pugnacious Republicans	123
VIII	Reconciliations	149
IX	Voices against Progress	171
Acknowledgments		205
Index		207

Introduction

Every autobiography that is worth its salt, or so a friend who read an earlier draft of this introduction observed, should have a distinctive quality, one that will make others want to immerse themselves in the tale being told. Looking for this *n'importe quoi*, I have reached for a suitable image for my life's journey. My individual human experience recalls the path of a particular train, one originally designed in the early nineteenth century, that goes from Strasburg, Pennsylvania, to nearby Paradise, and back again. This vehicle is not like the one described in Nathaniel Hawthorne's story "The Celestial Railroad." That imaginary vehicle was a symbol for human vanity and the promises of heaven on earth associated with technological advances. My train does not "thunder into the ancient city of Vanity," nor can anyone who has traveled on it believe that it will answer to all of his material needs once it has reached its destination across the Valley of Darkness.

This antique train keeps going back to its point of origin, and it does so again and again. But despite its predictable course, those who have been on board rave about their trip. They relive it in conversation for months. The train car, once it has left the remodeled Victorian-era station in Strasburg, meanders past fieldstone farms, modern shopping malls, and spruced-up eighteenth-century Pennsylvania Dutch villages. At the end of this voyage, it steams into its destination, a lumber yard in Paradise—where the train is readied for the return trip to Strasburg. In the summer, the rides feature concerts and food services, but whatever the added amenities, those who take the trip always believe they have been vouchsafed a unique experience by being able to travel on this historic vehicle.

What makes my life similar and perhaps even worth reading about is that it has gone nowhere in particular but has been nonetheless packed with fascinating encounters. Like the Strasburg train, others might find it riveting despite the absence of an inspiring direction. I recall sitting on the Strasburg train with my first wife and my late sister-in-law, both of whom died within a few months of our trip in 1994. It seems in retrospect that their journey to Paradise had been more than a tourist activity. For them the ride foreshadowed the impending end of their short lives; for me it signified the wheel of being, or some other ancient symbol of eternal recurrence. I returned to the beginning point of our trip, but not to a life that differed much from the one I had lived until then. That life, like the train, always brought me back to the same spot. The course of my journey was set decades ago.

There are two conditions that the reader will have to accept in order to appreciate what follows. One, this text does not aim at providing a comprehensive picture of my life. For those who are interested in the relevant biographical details, such data can be found interspersed in my *The Search for Historical Meaning* (1986) and in the entries under my name in *American Conservatism: An Encyclopedia* and *Who's Who in the World*. For those who know me and who pick up this book, the gaps that exist in the autobiographical sections scattered throughout will seem less troubling. Such readers will know how to connect the dotted lines that the disjointed references to my life might leave behind.

Two, this work deals specifically with my encounters with historically and intellectually significant dignitaries, a rule that, as I suggest, is not really violated in the discussion of my father, who rose to some eminence in his adopted land. Such a project required often painful selectivity, and the responsibility of choice did not always work to the benefit of my steadiest friends and closest relatives. Not all of these intimates made it into my tightly organized narrative. Another book, more plainly autobiographical, would be necessary in order to satisfy this demand for inclusiveness.

Two of the self-restricting rules that I accepted are that I would only treat family members in chapters 2 and 3, and that all of my other subjects would have to be older than I am and/or deceased. A less restrictive approach to my theme would have left my work less focused. It might have resulted in a book of thumbnail sketches of everyone I have known and liked. Certainly it would not have contributed to the development of a coherent narrative, which is what I was aiming for in this book.

This work is about what the title indicates and it is that by design. When the editors of ISI Books approached me three years ago and broached their plan for it, I accepted immediately. The reason is that the stimulating relations I have formed over the years should interest my readers far more than my undistinguished professional life. I have spent most of my career, as my discussion of the Strasburg train might suggest, as a detached loner working at small colleges in Illinois and Pennsylvania. Most of my life has been spent in the American East and in Rockford, Illinois, and I have achieved little in the way of local recognition in either place. My father and children have achieved perhaps more than I did socially and professionally.

My numerous works, as I mention in a later chapter, have generally been denied academic and journalistic attention. While this neglect may be at least partly attributed to my stormy relations with certain political factions, I suspect the explanation goes beyond that. I've been asking, from the perspective of the powers that be, the wrong kinds of questions, especially when I have turned my focus toward the contemporary world. The liberal establishment, or whatever establishment controls such matters, may have trouble dealing with someone who is imagined to inhabit a parallel universe. That may be in fact the way I'm perceived.

But the perplexity I've occasioned is definitely mutual: I've spent much of my adult life trying to understand those who have marginalized me, but I have done so with only limited success. My investigations of contemporary history have often seemed like journeys into someone else's era. Particularly obvious has been my alienation from today's youth culture. About two years ago, for example, while I was teaching a college class in Western civilization, I asked my students if they had heard of Julius Caesar. Only three of my thirty students answered that they had; and none admitted to having read a historical narrative before having been forced to take my course. Then I asked whether my students knew which group had been the most persecuted: women, gays, or blacks. A lively debate followed full of varied claims to victimhood. The sundry persecutions that my students cited were all supposedly connected in some fashion to a certain erstwhile junior senator from Wisconsin. In the 1950s, Joseph McCarthy had somehow managed to unleash harm against all minorities simultaneously. Although a stray fact might have been mixed into this gibberish, I have yet to determine what it was. Nor can I say that this litany of lamentation affected my students emotionally. Once it was over, they went back to jabbering on their cell phones and supplying each other with information about which designer's jeans were on sale at the local mall.

It might be argued that I am picking on very average young people by belaboring what they should not be expected to know. It is still possible, one might object, to find students at elite universities who would know what my students never bothered to learn. To this I would respond that I and the other members of my generation who took history classes at Bassick High School in Bridgeport, Connecticut, in the late 1950s would have been bored out of our minds by what I am now forced to teach students about Western civilization. Everyone in my high-school classes, and this includes those who never thought of going on to college, knew about ancient and medieval history. They were required to read Sir Walter Scott's *Ivanhoe* and several of Shakespeare's historical plays. These sons and daughters of immigrant factory workers in blue-collar Bridgeport were also made to think that it was their civilization they were learning about. Furthermore, when I studied Greek history in the ninth grade, my teacher Miss Maguire (I've no idea what her first name was) scolded me for not having identified enthusiastically enough with the Greeks when they were fighting the Persians. The students I now encounter in my nonage, with all due respect to Samuel Huntington, represent the "West" not at all. They are merely consumers who occupy the space of what used to be the Western world, and they fall over themselves trying to repudiate the "sexist, racist, anti-Semitic, and homophobic" culture that preceded them.

My students are certainly not the worst or the most incomprehensible of the younger generation. Even harder for me to appreciate is the IQ elite. While these people have mastered the technique of taking standardized exams and usually marry other members of what Richard Herrnstein and Charles Murray called, in *The Bell Curve*, the "cognitive elite," they intensely dislike the kind of Western culture that was here before their arrival in the world. Whether we are speaking about the promotion of anti-traditionalist social morality or the enlisting of public administration, the courts, and public education to advance multicultural agendas, traditional Westerners have much to fear from this gilded youth. Their cognitive skills show no connection to what the sociologist Will Herberg once characterized as "the funded wisdom of the ages."

Our cognitive elite has been happy to defend political censorship and social engineering. Its members have been conspicuously engaged in every effort to impose secularism and political correctness as a new civil religion. For all their test-taking intelligence, they are the last human beings I could imagine trying to preserve what was once understood as high culture. But then it is hard for me to understand what makes the rising generation tick—harder, that is to say, than being able to explain the nineteenth-century French bourgeoisie, Hellenistic historians, or other groups I have treated in my scholarship. Moreover, the contempt of the new elite for the old civilization has percolated downward with significant results. Just consider the attitudes of those who teach in our schools and of their not very bright students. What I have heard in my classes is presumably what professors at Harvard and Berkeley are able to say with less syntactical awkwardness. It is easy to trace how their rejection of gender roles and other inherited social arrangements (until recently thought to be rooted in nature) has played out at the bottom of the educational food chain. Noticing how our postbourgeois master class attracts intellectually insecure imitators has not enhanced my affection or respect for that group.

At the same time, some young academics have inspired me with slight hope for my profession. Last year at our college several of my thirtyish colleagues took the lead in blocking an attempt, spearheaded by certain administrators and the social-work department, to insert "multicultural" components into our core courses. The current chairwoman of our political-science department, who is several years younger than my two oldest children, took vigorous exception to this effort at a faculty meeting. When an administrator explained that the proposed reform was consistent with the "heritage of this school," as a German Anabaptist institution, my colleague responded that she could not find a single trace of such a tradition in the institutional past. The original mission statement had referred to Christ and not to lifestyle diversity.

I'm also reminded of those interested and principled students I have taught over the years: the book-reading, contentious high-school teachers who took a stimulating evening graduate class with me at NYU in 1971; a former student from Rockford College, now a middle-aged lawyer, who keeps steadily in touch; a Vietnamese girl at Elizabethtown whom her adopted parents rescued from the rubble of her native land and who studies day and night. Most recently I have taken pedagogic pride in the actions of an independent-minded graduating senior who took several of my classes, including classical Greek. This student, Corey Thomas, was president of his senior class and as such received the privilege of addressing us at commencement. Unlike others who have enjoyed this honor, Corey had something substantive to say about the topic "celebrating who we are." And he did not approach his subject in a politically prescribed way. Instead, he dwelled on the virtues of his New England Puritan ancestors and of those entrepreneurial Welsh relatives on his father's side who had founded and run mines in northern Pennsylvania. He referred to his doughty Presbyterian grandfather, who had idolized Robert Taft and who had died the previous year. Corey stressed that while he was certainly not denigrating anyone else's ancestors, he had a moral duty to "celebrate" his own and their now fading political and moral world.

A feminist Pecksniff told Corey, when she heard what he intended to say, that he was not upholding our school's dedication to "diversity." He wisely ignored her counsels, and I let him know after his speech that his remarks came closer than anything I had heard since 1965 to being an act of WASP self-validation. That was the year of my last visit to the Yale Elizabethan Club, a stuffy rallying point for bookish WASPs of a traditionalist bent who met on Tuesday afternoons to eat tasteless cucumber sandwiches and to note who in their society had "gone into business." The difference of course was that Corey, unlike these quaint snobs, was providing a now badly needed defense of the collective honor of his and their ancestors.

It is not a matter of indifference that those who first settled the U.S. and gave this land its political and religious character have denigrated themselves and their history. In fact, those who shared Corey's white Protestant background went ballistic over his modest defense of WASPdom. This calls to mind the recent efforts made by one-time Democratic presidential hopeful John Edwards to play the race card—against his own race. Edwards's efforts to make (white) racism into a central issue of his campaign only validated the anti-WASP hysteria prevalent among academics and journalists.

Despite my occasionally happy memories of colleagues and students, it is obvious that I have not fitted into my profession snugly. Each time I think about this, I recall a particular movie that I have watched more often than most of the other films in my wife's VHS repertoire: *Being There* (1979). What once most amused me about this Peter Sellers movie, scripted by the talented but mentally and morally unstable Jerzy Koszinski, was the depiction of its key figure, a long-secluded gardener who rises to power and influence owing to a series of misimpressions. Having lived in Washington, it dawned on me that this spoof about a simpleton (played by Sellers) mistaken for an international-relations expert was not far off the mark. But as I watched the film several more times, the lines that stayed with me longest were the ones uttered by the millionaire husband of actress Shirley MacLaine, played by Melvyn Douglas. This ailing business tycoon gives instructions that at his funeral someone read a few thoughts he has scribbled down for posterity. One of his observations is the following: "I have known a lot of common working people, who also knew me. And I can't say we've liked each other." My older son and I laugh uproariously each time we hear that line. But in my case the laughter is caused by the fact that the passage epitomizes my professional relations. I have indicated to my family that I would like those lines read at my gravesite, but with the appropriate substitution of academics for working men.

Being There has caused me to reflect on some of my professional-networking failures. Many of my colleagues and I have not clicked, and the reason may be a difference in sensibility. Although I courted well-placed academics and enjoyed the smells and sounds of famous universities in my younger years, as I have grown older I have developed a distaste for academic culture. More precisely, I have developed a Nietzschean reaction to the girly men and virago women that populate university settings. There is for me something deeply unpleasant about such environments, although perhaps I'm reacting to these annoyances far more than I should. When I met Beverly Jarrett, the gracious former director of the University of Missouri Press, two years ago at the annual meeting of the American Political Science Association in Philadelphia, I began raging at the sight of the mannish women and mincing feminized males, all of whom were dressed with the sartorial gracelessness of a televangelist. Although my interlocutor agreed that "they do look weird," she may have been only trying to be polite.

Thrust among these creatures, however, I came to appreciate the very normal and even heroic human beings whose lives have intersected with mine. I thought often about my father, who exemplified manliness and generosity, and about my dedicated mother and my late wife Dana, who would have walked through fire for their children. I also reflected on Dana's parents, who lived for their daughter, someone who died while still young but not without having imitated her progenitors' model of sacrifice in her relations to her five children. I have also considered the example of my eldest daughter and her husband, who must deal with a severely disabled child every day of their lives. Those shallow careerists and feminist ranters who cause me to reach for Rolaids have served to point me in the direction of those who deserve my respect, despite the perceptible fact that this book does not do the latter group full justice. Ancient Jewish leaders warned their flock not to imitate the Egyptians, who would have coarsened their sense of propriety. But knowing whose example we should shun also teaches us to recognize whom or what we should admire. This may have been the most significant consequence of my generally unrewarding professional career: I have come to appreciate the superior human qualities of certain nonacademics, or of those who were academics in the same way that Dr. Johnson characterized the Toryism of David Hume, that is, by accident.

In my early fifties, after I had been widowed in Lancaster, Pennsylvania, with several dependent children, I decided that I would no longer seek academic advancement. Since the train kept going back to the same spot, why place any hope in the unlikely possibility that it would go somewhere else the next time around? Besides tending to my domestic obligations, I quietly taught my classes at Elizabethtown College, which as far as I could tell was the only college that would have me. I also continued to write articles and books, with the hope rather than expectation that some later generation would take my thought seriously. But most importantly, I sought out those people of substance who could bear my company. All of them, in different ways, were necessarily outsiders, even if one of them, Richard Nixon, had been president of the United States. Although the same people continued to direct the Strasburg train service, I discovered that it was possible to enjoy the scenery without having to drag my aging body back on the train. One could simply drive into the country at one's leisure—and not worry about specific rides and schedules. That is, one could cultivate instructive and pleasant friendships without thinking of oneself as an academic on a conveyor belt. The historian John Lukacs once said to me, with reference to his lengthy teaching career at Chestnut Hill College, "If you and I were teaching history at Harvard, it is we who would have to worry about our integrity." My response to John was that "happily, we won't have to worry about that."

The purpose of this observation is to point out what for me has been a cause for hope. It is entirely possible to pursue a fruitful scholarly career and to meet noteworthy people without having to truckle to a Byzantine academic hierarchy. Although I would not recommend following in my footsteps to my own flesh and blood, one can survive at the margins of academia while being out of sync with its monolithic culture. I cite my life—and that of John Lukacs—as a case in point. This book recalls my encounters with other such professorial nonconformists, figures who have represented the true dissenting academy.

RICHARD NIXON

577 CHESTNUT RIDGE ROAD
WOODCLIFF LAKE, NEW JERSEY

9-12-'92

Dear Paul,

Just a note to tell you that I found Forrest + Ellen McDonald's Requiem one of the most perceptive commentaries on the early days of the nation I have ever read. The speech format makes it much easier for non experts in the field to understand. I particularly liked the way they demolished some of conventional myths about the men + the events.

I look forward to seeing you next month

Sincerely

RN

I

Apam

My father was not the nicest person I have known. His foul temper became legendary in our family; and despite his middling physical appearance and a bald pate that he had acquired in his thirties, he continued to pride himself on his supposed good looks well into his late fifties. Beside such self-sacrificing types as my late wife Dana and her parents, who had survived the horrors of the Nazi and Soviet occupations of Poland without losing their uncommon humanity and benevolence, my father was a conventionally flawed person. He held grudges with extraordinary tenacity, and he never let us forget who had done him dirt.

One can, however, credit him with at least equally extraordinary positive qualities. He would have given his shirt away in a fit of generosity; and despite my mother's stern warnings, he was always lavishing money on his relatives, none of whom had done as well as he had in the New World. He displayed extraordinary talent in the applied sciences; he not only built and wired additions to the house in which I grew up, when he was already in his late sixties, but he also designed apparatus for the Bridgeport (CT) Fire Department. For many years he served on the municipal Fire Commission and as an ex officio member of the Police Commission, and he shone on these boards as an authority distinguished in certain technical fields. He assumed these public responsibilities in response to a request from the Republican mayor of Bridgeport, Nick Panuzio, who had known and respected my father while the mayor was still a boy.

In terms of his fiery courage, my father had nothing in common with today's feminized and media-acceptable males. While recently engrossed in R. Cort Kirkwood's *Real Men: Ten Courageous Americans to Know and Admire* (2006), I thought of how closely my father resembled the military heroes portrayed therein. Unlike George Patton, George Washington, and Robert E. Lee, my father had not distinguished himself as a soldier. But in his readiness to risk his life as a matter of honor, he did not differ much from Kirkwood's exemplars of valor. Once, when he was already advanced in years and in visibly failing health, several local toughs, who had followed my parents back from a shopping mall, broke into their house and held them up at knife point. When they ordered my father to lie down on the floor, he responded, "The hell I will." Picking up a nearby antique lamp, he smashed it over the head of one of the three robbers. Another one delivered a glancing punch, which my father mostly avoided before striking his assailant back. Thereupon the robbers ran out of the house with my father in frenzied pursuit. The next day Dad picked up information about those who had come to rob him and my mother from the local police. It seems that these malefactors had been arrested for other break-ins but those who actually had evidence of their crimes had been too frightened to press charges. My father made sure they were rearrested and then formally accused them of breaking into his house with the intent to rob. He also told his former assailants that if he saw them prowling around his neighborhood again he'd be delighted to kill them with the gun he stored upstairs.

Needless to say, my father suffered in no way from the politics of guilt. He refused to work any further with the Fire Commission when he learned that it had established lower standards for black applicants on the entry exam. He also urged the fire captain to stay out of certain minority-occupied projects, in which the inhabitants had a tendency to pelt firefighters with stones and trash. My father's characteristic response was "Let the troublemakers who lit the fire get burnt." Although a refugee from the Nazis who probably lost family members in the Holocaust (he could never determine with any certitude how his half-brother and his children had perished during the war), Dad would go ballistic if someone tried to misapply the "lessons" of Nazi genocide. He never blamed American Christians for what had been done by European Nazis; and he grew particularly exasperated if someone tried to draw dishonest implications from what had befallen Nazi victims. He did not think that the American civil-rights revolution was "mandated" by events that unfolded in Hitler's Germany or Stalin's Russia; and he would go speechless with rage if someone suggested that "Jews are morally required" to support a porous border with Latin America because a ship full of German Jews had not been allowed into the U.S. in 1940. In his view, such contrived parallels were utterly specious. They were made to fit a contemporary political agenda—one that my father definitely did not support.

By now, it should be clear why I have singled out my father for special treatment in this chapter. For he was the person who influenced me most decisively in terms of my own outlook and sentiments. When I was a child, my mother accounted for my stubborn, rebellious streak by reminding her relatives that I was "my father's son." My history department chairman at Case Western Reserve once referred jokingly to my father, after he had met him at my home, as "little Paul."

On one big issue we disagreed, but I never pushed my father very hard to justify himself because I enjoyed the reasons he gave for his predilection. He adored FDR, and periodically he would take my brother and me to tour the Roosevelt estate at Hyde Park, New York. Once there, he would lapse into rhapsodies about the achievements of the president, who is buried behind his ancestral home, overlooking the Hudson, next to the remains of his Scottie Fala. Although "naïve about Stalin," FDR had kept Hitler, who "took countries like a drunken maniac," from overrunning Europe and from killing all of my father's relatives. Beyond his attainments in international affairs, FDR had done "some good things" at home, although the list of such accomplishments, even in Dad's telling, was extremely limited. They consisted of closing the banks when he took office and his bold decision to take derelicts off the street and to send them to work camps. My father viewed FDR as the American counterpart of a European strongman, an authoritarian leader who avoided the excesses of Hitler and Stalin but who meant business when he addressed staggering economic problems. An American libertarian would have struck my father as being at least as strange as a feminist or an advocate of the civil-rights revolution. In contrast to those who define themselves as economic conservatives but social liberals, Dad was socially on what today would be the far Right, but he was equally open to some kind of national welfare state. His views were those of an interwar European rather than of an American in the early twenty-first century.

Born in Budapest on December 24, 1911, my father felt comfortable in a world of fixed authorities, albeit one in which as a boy he had stood at the outer edge. His mother's family had been affluent, assimilated Austrian Jews; my grandmother came from Graz, the capital of Styria, which as fate would have it, I visited as the guest of my German publisher, Leopold Stocker Verlag, in the summer of

2006. But my grandmother had abandoned her first husband and my uncle Emil for a tailor she had met in Vienna; and the two had gone off together to the Hungarian capital, which was then a still largely German-speaking city, and one in which my grandparents failed to prosper. The irregular relation between Paul (my grandfather) and Dorothea (my grandmother), both of whom had forsaken their earlier households, and Paul's wastrel habits resulted in poverty and social exclusion for their three children—of whom my father Andrew was the youngest. Dad's early years must be understood in light of these social circumstances, a situation that undoubtedly shaped his later attitudes. His concern with structures of authority might have been affected by the fact that he grew up as an outcast within his mother's family and in the broader society. Most of his adult life was spent working his way into bourgeois respectability, first in Europe and then, from the late '30s on, in the United States.

His childhood was marred by memories of war, defeat, and popular turmoil. As he often told me, his first school became a hospital for wounded soldiers from the Austro-Hungarian army during the First World War. After his country had lost that struggle and suffered occupation, a Communist revolution broke out in 1919, resulting in the establishment of the ill-fated and inept Bela Kun regime; this disaster then made way for a rightist regency under Admiral Miklos Horthy, which the Allies helped to install in a strife-ridden Hungary. Every change seemed in my father's young mind to bring increased problems, going from human loss to Communist violence to a dishonest and intermittently anti-Semitic government, pretending to stand for the defeated Hungarians but really shilling for Hungary's enemies. Despite these disagreeable circumstances, my father prospered as a master furrier; his impoverished family had had him apprenticed in this once lucrative trade, and he was able to rise through the ranks through examinations. By the time he had reached his mid-twenties and had become the owner of a store in a plush commercial sector of Pest, he was, from all accounts, leading the life of a bon vivant.

My father decided to come to the United States for two reasons. The first was that after the assassination of the Austrian Chancellor Engelbert Dollfuss in July 1934 at the hands of Nazi agents, he assumed that it was only a matter of time before Hitler "liberated" the Alpine Republic and integrated Austria into the new German Reich. He had no doubt that the Nazi government was as bad as it was rumored to be, and paramilitary groups that imitated the German Nazis were already operating in Hungary, a problem that the authoritarian regime of Horthy became increasingly powerless to deal with. There was also a large underground Communist Party, which was subservient to Moscow and looked back on the expropriations and summary executions of the Kun interlude with undisguised nostalgia. My father properly surmised that Hungary, and East Central Europe in general, would soon be the plaything of rival tyrannies; it was therefore best to get out while he still had time.

The second reason was that my father's older sister, Regina, was married to a formerly poor Hungarian Jewish sharecropper who apparently had struck it rich in the New World. Regina's husband Morris, as luck would have it, had been born in the U.S. while his parents were briefly sojourning there at the beginning of the twentieth century. Somehow this American-born brother-in-law had managed to bring my grandmother to New York, a fate that she bitterly lamented. She had been uprooted twice, she complained, and having left Austria for Hungary, where the people spoke some kind of weird Turkic language, she now found herself among the "*ungezogene Kinder* [badly behaved children]" of Anglophone America. My aunt and uncle convinced her not to go back to the brewing cauldron of

Central Europe; and they made her continued stay more bearable by helping to "bring out" in rapid succession my father, my uncle Jenö (Eugene), and Jenö's comely wife Dora.

Unlike his brother and mother, my father adjusted quickly to his new environment. He began to learn English, which he mastered except for his tendency to substitute German possessive pronouns (e.g., *mein Car*) for English ones. He also obtained employment as a furrier, repairing coats for large fur dealers. But he had to change jobs periodically because of his lack of "a red book." Apparently only bona fide Communist Party members were supposed to work in these shops, and my father, who found the Communists to be vulgar and annoying, refused to join their movement. At one point he had to hide on a fire escape when the Communist organizer came into his place of work in order to check on the party membership of the employees. Dad was warned that party thugs had a way of punishing nonmembers who presumed to work in a "party shop." Immediately afterwards he changed his place of employment by going to work for a large fur business in Bridgeport, Connecticut; and once he had collected enough capital there, he opened his own shop.

Although my father was a loner who read Hungarian literature and did complicated home repairs during his leisure hours, he somehow found time to meet and marry my mother. My maternal grandfather was the uncle of Regina's husband Morris, and he showed himself to be extremely hospitable to my father, who visited him soon after arriving in the U.S. Papa (my grandfather) was hard-working and frugal to a fault; he would walk from his nearby apartment to the fur dye factory that he owned in Green Point, near the Brooklyn Naval Yards, rather than spend a few cents on a street car. He believed that that the pennies added up—especially if one had to go to work at least six days a week. Besides, exercise, as he saw it, was good for the body, particularly if it resulted in money in the bank. My grandmother would wake up no later than 3:00 A.M. to prepare her husband's breakfast and lunch, and Papa would be off to work before sunrise. During the day he would do the heavy lifting in his factory because, as he explained to us, he didn't want to deal with unionized workers. Better, he thought, to drag around heavy barrels of chemicals at age seventy or seventy-five, with finger nails disfigured by dyes, than to have to rely on whiny union men.

To his credit, he made sure that the three of his five offspring who survived early childhood studied useful vocations. My aunt, who was eleven years older than my mother, became an accountant, a profession that she practiced for almost sixty years, even after her husband, who flitted from one job to the next, had retired. My mother's younger brother went to college intending to study medicine but then got married at age twenty and transferred to pharmacy. My mother, Ruth, was sent to a toney business college but never established herself as a legal secretary, because she married my father and produced an obstreperous son (me) about a year and a half later. Although my grandparents' friends had children studying the "humanities" at universities, my grandfather viewed this path as frivolous. He thought that a young person should go to school to "provide for a family" and not to traffic in ideas. Least of all did one want adolescent children coming home from college talking about revolution, a silly pastime that interfered with getting a job and settling down.

Papa took instantly to my father, who came to visit a few weeks after he had arrived in New York, and who bedazzled his distant relative through marriage with Old World savoir-faire. My mother likewise fell for this visitor, although he was "much older," by seven and a half years, and was imagined to have led a much livelier and perhaps more "questionable" social life in Europe than my mother, who was just graduating from high school, could imagine. The couple was married about five years later, after what was considered a proper courtship. I suspect that my grandfather, among other things, wanted to make sure that his prospective son-in-law was a solid type—and not like most of Dad's kin, who eschewed hard work.

What no one fully grasped was that the home my parents would go on to set up would include some of my father's immigrant relatives, and most disturbingly my paternal grandmother, who ruled like a Chinese matriarch. I respect my mother deeply for having put up with this forbidding lady, and above all with the unpleasantness of having to listen to her rail against American social immorality. For years after her mother-in-law's death in 1943, my mother would complain about the older woman's annoying hypocrisy. Although herself not exactly a paradigm of bourgeois virtues, she condemned those in whose country she had taken refuge for being self-indulgent. Even so, my father's mother cared for me as an infant, and she regaled me with Austrian songs that undoubtedly put me to sleep despite my bouts of infantile colic.

My father became a constant companion to his father-in-law, who survived the deaths of two sickly wives and eventually came to live with us. I have never known a more dutiful son-in-law than my father became in looking after my ailing and eventually senile grandfather. It was as if he felt a deep debt of gratitude to this man who had given him his daughter as a wife when he was but a newly arrived immigrant. He may likewise have seen in his father-in-law a substitute father for the one who had bestowed little attention on his children before smoking himself to death.

My father always included Papa when he took me and my brother on Sunday outings in his early-1950s vintage Pontiac. These trips would invariably last four to five hours and involved visiting some nearby Connecticut town or chugging along Route 7, which hugged the state line with New York. On special occasions, for which we eagerly planned, we would travel as far as Boston, Philadelphia, or Hyde Park, but we would always come back the same day. And we would usually bring along a basket full of sandwiches, prepared by my mother, consisting of roast beef or turkey from Friday evening's meal. There were also summer trips, which my grandfather did not join because of his deteriorating health; these would carry our family to such northern destinations as Montreal, Quebec City, or Niagara Falls. One of two contemporaries of mine, Sam Goldberger or my cousin Susan, would come along on these journeys; and although both are now world travelers well into their sixties, they still recall these trips of their youth more fondly than any of the journeys they have taken since. Significantly, my father would never stay away from his work or from Bridgeport for more than a few days. His first major trip after many decades spent in the U.S. was back to his native city, whither he traveled in the mid-1960s. He was not especially impressed by what he saw. Budapest under Communist rule, he told us, looked like a much shabbier place than Paris, Vienna, Jerusalem, or any of the other foreign cities he thereafter visited.

It may behoove me to protect my father from a charge leveled against him by my mother. Dad was considered to be a spendthrift who would have left his family with little if anything had he died in his forties or fifties. Here a distinction may be in order between the generosity (*eleutheriotes*) that Aristotle thought was worthy of a free man (*eleutheroprepes*) and the habits of a wastrel. My father's giving fell into the first category, one that Aristotle never viewed as excessive and which he famously praised as an aristocratic trait in the *Nicomachean Ethics*. Dad was generous to relatives, and he hastened to help out the family of his older brother when my uncle fell ill with terminal lung cancer. He would also receive house guests with effusive hospitality, and when I was a graduate student at Yale, both of my parents would invite home for dinner my classmates and their spouses. My father was particularly kind to one of my older classmates, who could never muster the energy to finish his dissertation on the Assyrian concept of time. This friend, Laszlo, came from a distinguished Hungarian family that had held high positions in the Horthy government. Unfortunately, this offspring of distinguished Hungarian gentry was a nervous, diminutive man who chain-smoked and could never put his life in order. Each time he tried to describe to me his puzzling dissertation topic, Laszlo would plunge into a state of nervous exhaustion.

When it came to reaching decisions, my father was eminently practical. While my brother Sam graduated at the top of their classes at Bassick High School in Bridgeport, I was a less disciplined student who barely made it onto the bottom of the honor's list. When it came to a choice of colleges, my brother was taken at Cornell; his achievement was comparable to that of Sam, who a few years earlier had made it into Yale. But as a less driven student I ended up going to Yeshiva University, a school that accepted me with a partial scholarship. To make a long story even longer: my younger brother, who majored in physics, decided in his senior year to go to medical school. Five years earlier I had made a markedly different and less lucrative turn when I had spurned a chance to attend NYU Law School in favor of Yale graduate school. Although my father placed no pressure on his sons in terms of career decisions, I suspect he thought that my brother had chosen more wisely. A girl whom I was then going with broke off relations as soon as she had learned of my foolhardy professional decision. Neither my brother nor I was showered with goodies while in school. Unlike the pampered students I have taught in recent years, we lived by current standards of student life in a Third World fashion. We also believed that we owed what we had to our parents, in contrast to the students whom I encounter nowadays who shamelessly complain that their parents didn't do enough to provide them with "self-esteem."

Looking at my parents, I devised the theory of "aesthetic equivalence," a notion that I have been teaching to my students for over thirty years. Most couples I have observed over the years are roughly equivalent in terms of physical attractiveness. Young people develop an intuitive sense of their relative marketability in appealing to the opposite sex, and the reason that plain-looking couples are so often happy with each other is that they understand the limits of their physical attributes. Equally important, they incorporate a consciousness of these limits in choosing significant others. Although other variables may contribute to such selection, aesthetic equivalence is usually a powerful explanation in ascertaining why particular young men and women have teamed up. When one therefore encounters a highly attractive man or woman married to a less physically appealing mate, one looks for special factors that might have affected this unusual selection. This puzzlement is especially appropriate in modern Western society, in which marriages are not arranged and in which few young people have to conform to extraneous social pressures.

In my parents' case there was a degree of aesthetic disparity that I noticed even as a pre-adolescent. My mother, quite simply, was much better looking than my father. She had a delicate bone structure and a sweet, girlish face well into her sixties, when a number of illnesses began to damage her erstwhile Mary Pickford appearance. Until then Mom had aged more slowly than her spouse and, besides that, she was almost eight years younger. But unlike most other men, and particularly those in European Jewish communities I have met,

Dad had a sense of presence. He also had loads of Old World charm, a quality that was similar to the intoxicant that my Greek friend the witty columnist Taki Theodoracopulos exudes. (He failed, however, to bequeath this special charm to his two painfully sedate sons.) My late wife Dana commented on this magnetic quality when she first met my father in 1968. She found him initially far more pleasing than my mother (although the two eventually became close friends) because of his attentiveness to women, particularly those whom he was encountering for the first time. He was also a splendid ballroom dancer, unlike his two sons, who have drawn whispers on the dance floor by being flat-footed embarrassments.

But it was my father's sense of command, what the Romans called *auctoritas*, that stood out most distinctly among his positive qualities. Bridgeport had a large Hungarian-speaking community, and one of the reasons that my father and his family had settled there was the possibility of conducting business in Hungarian while working to pick up English. My father spoke the best Hungarian and the worst German in his family. This was the result of three factors: his extensive education in Hungarian, his reluctance to respond to his mother *auf deutsch*, and his impressive knowledge of Hungarian letters and history.

Dad developed extensive social and commercial contacts with the large Hungarian Jewish community in Bridgeport; and although he only attended religious services on special occasions a few times a year, he joined their synagogue on the west side of our then bustling Connecticut industrial hub, in what was called "Hunkeytown." The congregation had been founded in 1909 by "young men from Hungary," as the synagogue's charter explained. The founders had almost all gone back to Europe afterwards and had fought in the Austro-Hungarian army during World War I. Many returned to Bridgeport years later, after various odysseys in South America and Europe. My childhood buddy Sam Goldberger, who grew up in that community and spoke Hungarian and some German before learning English in school, is preparing a social history of our once flourishing but now vanished *gemeinschaft*. Within it, my father was accorded respect as a man of some standing, and people would come to our house seeking his advice about personal and business matters alike. Although largely self-educated, he seemed by the standards of a transplanted peasant culture to be someone who truly stood apart from the others.

Years later, when my brother drew a distinction between our immigrant father and my brother's wife's parents, who had attended prestigious American universities generations ago, I could not grasp how our father had occupied a lower social level. He seemed in my view to have done better than I did; if nothing else, his name is on the cornerstones of the firehouses in Bridgeport, where he distinguished himself as a public servant. In the Hungarian community he was always respectfully addressed as *Gottfried Úr*, a term that suggested something more exalted than "Mister" but did not quite indicate gentry stock. Others of peasant origin (*parasztság*) were referred to as *bácsi* and *néni*, uncle and aunt, terms that were also used to cover all blood relatives of an older generation. Although I recall addressing my father as Dad or, when I was younger, as Daddy, my relatives tried to get me to think of him as *apám*. This was the Hungarian word for father, an expression that I never grew accustomed to. This was because my father had spoken to his sons in English, while his mother, who had looked after me as a small child, had communicated in Austrian German. As a result, I never mastered more than a few simple phrases in Hungarian, while to this day I speak German like a pre–World War I Viennese.

My father's *auctoritas* was on display once when the mayor asked him for a particular favor. His district was about to hold an election for alderman, and since the Republican Party would likely pick up the seat on the city council, it was imperative to find a candidate who would vote with the Republican mayor. Nick asked Dad to come up with the name of some lawyer in his neighborhood whom he thought might fit the bill. My father settled on a young, recently married lawyer whose parents he had known well; and he told this youthful lawyer, Burton, to come by the house to speak to him. When Burton arrived and my father asked if he would like to be alderman, his young house guest began to get chummy, calling his host by his nickname "Andy," and then launching into a speech about how he would "improve this place" once elected. My father scowled at him and proceeded to lay down the law: He was Commissioner Gottfried, and not Andy, to someone who was younger by several years than my younger brother.

Moreover, if Burton wanted the nod for the Republican nomination, he would have to promise not "to yap about naïve programs," but to vote with Mayor Panuzio. The Republican Party was looking for a safe vote and not for a TV commentator.

My father's *auctoritas* became less impressive as he aged. In his mid-sixties he fell into an unseemly quarrel with Dana's father while both were visiting us in Rockford. My wife and I understood what was taking place: Our fathers had been hard, resourceful men whose sense of self-worth was growing more brittle as they became older. They also had drunk more of the Scotch my father-in-law had brought from Toronto than they should have. Afterwards, while working to set up a swing set for our youngsters in the backyard, they began to raise their voices in an unfriendly manner. By late afternoon they were insulting one another, and only by separating them did we avoid a further escalation of hostilities. By evening, the storm had passed; nonetheless, I don't remember seeing Dad and my father-in-law show much in the way of friendship toward each other again. By then both were exhibiting the effects of too much drinking and of a certain noticeable arterial deterioration. What had angered Dana's father, a generally dignified physician with vast humanistic learning, were my father's boastful expressions of self-importance. Twenty or even ten years earlier I could not have imagined him acting in this manner. As a younger man, he had taken his talents in stride and would have been irritated by the same behavior that my father-in-law had loudly berated him for.

During the last ten years of his life, my father exhibited a certain erratic quality that made it hard for my five children, including the two oldest ones, to imagine him as he had once been. By the time he died of congestive heart failure in 1987, he had become a shell of his former self, and it was only by virtue of my age that I could remember him as someone who had once been far more impressive, an authority figure who soared above his companions. I remember my own sense of disbelief when he visited me for the last time, after we had moved from Rockford to a Washington suburb. By then Dad was doddering and quite deaf, and it was hard for me to associate him with the Titan I had once relied on. Then the unexpected happened. Our basement began to fill up with water when one of the spring downpours, so common in the Washington suburbs, wrought havoc to our property. Whereupon my father ran down to the basement and found a sump pump, which he got to work. Before long he had organized me and my five children for the purpose of lugging pails of muddy water from the lower level up to the front door. From there we had to pull our loads over to the road, so that the water we emptied would not seep back into the basement. Within an hour my father had the problem under control. By the next morning the basement was almost dry, except for the musty odor that was always present and made it almost uninhabitable.

The water would return to our basement the following week, when the next downpour occurred. But the beautiful part of the incident was that it allowed my family and me to see my father one last time as he had once been—as someone obviously in command. Even in his final months, as his energy ebbed, his old and truest self shined through.

Robert Nisbet
2828 Wisconsin Avenue, N. W.
Washington, D. C. 20007

September 17, 1986

Dear Paul:

You were very kind to have a copy of your The Search for Historical Meaning sent to me, and I've just finished reading its extremely captivating text. You've told me much about the present I somehow had not before come across. And I particularly relish your treatment of Leo Straus. I never much liked him---I met him once in the early '60s in a small group in Chicago for a long evening---and I have resented him on his ignorant comments on not only Burke but Max Weber. On the other hand I do have to respect him for some of his enemies.

And your section on the Neos in the latest The World & I is sparkling, beginning with your own essay---the best of them, I thought. You are already making a difference in Washington.

Best,

BN

II

A Life Recalled

My introduction dwells on a metaphor that compares my life to the tourist train that returns again and again to its point of origin in Strasburg, Pennsylvania. While this description fits certain aspects of my life and suggests its static quality, it does not take into account the changes that have also marked my existence. Least of all does the metaphor indicate the benefits that resulted from my relations to family members, people who influenced my development in many positive ways. Without their ministrations my life would have been socially less rich and far less pleasant. At the top of this list, chronologically, stand my parents, who were introduced in the previous chapter. Both were preoccupied with me and my younger brother and tried to chart our futures in just about the same way that I would later do for my five children. They warned me against entering a profession in which "you have to depend on someone else," and I did the same for my offspring, who are now mostly in their thirties. They heard from me the same warning I had received from my parents: "Don't go into anything that requires you to grovel in order to get ahead!"

I got this lesson across to my children a bit more effectively than my parents did, at least in my case. My eldest daughter, Barbara, finished her graduate studies as an econometrician before she married and had children. Despite her trying family schedule, Barbara has pursued a lucrative avocation as the author of mathematics textbooks and standardized exams. My older son, Joseph, who was a student nonpareil, is both a physician and a corporate lawyer. My third son, Jonathan, is also a corporate lawyer, but one who feels free to change his position periodically if he tires of his work situation. My middle daughter, Beth, who is married without children, has held various editing positions but has never felt under any constraint to stay in a job she dislikes. She has also published a sprightly book with Penguin on popular culture, one that has probably sold more briskly than any of my publications, save for the first edition of *The Conservative Movement* (1988). Although my youngest daughter Sara still has to "shape up," my late wife's term for the maturation process, I continue to hope that she'll do well as a businesswoman. Since her mother died when she was only eight, Sara has had a long row to hoe, but her social effusiveness and love of commerce may serve her well. My one satisfaction as I observe my children's progress is that none of them imitated my dubious example, for I chose a vocation that, contrary to my parents' wise admonitions, has left me at the mercy of others, and often at the mercy of those who do not wish me well.

Although my parents always meant to do what was best for me, they inadvertently worsened my adolescence by feeding me to excess. The steady diet of Central European cuisine caused me to bulk out as a teenager, with the result that I had to endure endless ridicule from my high-school classmates. I recall a photograph of myself taken just before my bar mitzvah, a Jewish rite of passage signaling the beginning of male adulthood. I am so obese that even fifty years later, it is hard for me to gaze at this old photo without wincing. Although I have been as thin as a rail since my late teens, the picture evokes memories of adolescent awkwardness and of being bullied by less ungainly classmates.

This situation may have been one of the reasons that I consented to attend Yeshiva University, an institution at which I expected to find lots of nonthreatening geeks. That was exactly what I found, but there were complications I had not reckoned on. As soon as I arrived, I felt a massive cultural barrier separating me from my new classmates, who were preponderantly from Brooklyn and Queens, had attended one of several Orthodox Jewish schools, and seemed to carry with them the social gracelessness of having grown up in a transported Eastern European ghetto. They were also, not incidentally, naturally bright, and they did well on premed exams, mathematical exercises, and, to the extent they took this work seriously, the study of ancient and medieval rabbinic glosses. They also showed a clannishness that extended even to their fellow Jews. The few Sephardic and more numerous Austro-German Jews in their midst, even if they came from "the City," had trouble fitting into the dominant society.

One occasion for cultural clashes was the election held for school offices. The inside group always picked its own slate of candidates, and they were usually destined to win. But one year the outsiders decided to run me along with a few of my colleagues as an alternative slate. It is hard to tell whether I really received no more than one-third of the votes tabulated, since the insiders had not bothered to vote in the expected numbers. But there were also knavish tricks that had been allowed to go on, including ballot-stuffing. When I asked one of my fellow outsiders, a German Jew from Washington Heights (then a German Jewish enclave in Upper Manhattan), what he thought about the outcome, he shrugged his shoulders and mumbled the word "democracy." To this day I can't figure out whether he was praising the election or simply being cynical.

During my first two years of college, I looked for ways of getting out, going home on weekends and inquiring at universities in the New York–Connecticut area where I could transfer without losing too many credits. Since a certain percentage of our work had to be taken in specifically Jewish subjects, like Talmud, it became progressively difficult to transfer to another institution without having to forfeit more credits than I was willing to give up. My religious beliefs seemed less and less to resemble those of my classmates, a fact that I noticed during my college years. I had never really been an Orthodox Jew, even if I had been a conventionally observant one. At the same time, I did keep traditional Jewish dietary and other Rabbinic laws, although never with the rigor displayed by my Orthodox associates. These laws were for me mainly an ethnic and cultural point of reference. I could not relate them to a well-developed theology, as opposed to an ad hoc justification for ordering one's communal life in accordance with certain Rabbinic teachings. By the time I was in my third year of college, I had come close to accepting, without knowing it, Spinoza's scheme of human spiritual Progress, from the Mosaic code through the visions of universalist prophets, like Isaiah, to the teachings of Jesus.

What distinguished my thinking from this evolutionary scheme, however, was that I also profoundly revered the Old Testament Deity, the God of thunder and judgment, although not the proliferating ancient and medieval Rabbinic glosses that His Jewish worshippers had produced on His behalf. I could never quite bring myself to become a Protestant, although I resonated to what the Reformers had said about the dialectic between faith and the law. God for me was the Hebrew one, who existed in splendid, transcendent Otherness. It was inconceivable for me that He would have condescended to have himself tortured to death in order to atone for "our sins."

That said, I had never been attracted to a life of endless ritual founded on Rabbinic legal decisions and to be lived in a closed social environment. This opinion is not intended to belittle anyone but rather reflects my Western understanding of religious thinking. I would not hide from my readers the cultural orientation from which it springs. It is a cultural predisposition that allows me to appreciate the theological reasoning of Aquinas or Luther more than it does certain other forms of religious exposition—for example, the legal exegesis of third-century Babylonian Jews interpreting the sequence of rituals for carrying out animal sacrifices.

Yet Jewish ritual life has obvious communal value, as I already recognized while at Yeshiva University. It held together a dispersed people in the face of oppression, even if the laws and the resulting isolation created difficulties for traditional Jews with their gentile neighbors. There was likewise cohesion and a sense of warmth in the Jewish society I observed, and I noted that my mother, who in my teens had gravitated toward a Hungarian Orthodox community in Bridgeport, found among her new friends a social ambience that gave her daily life, particularly after her children had grown up, sustained meaning.

What the philosopher Thomas Molnar once said to me about Carl Schmitt—that "he was a Catholic without being a Christian"—might be applied to my relations with my fellow Jews. I have always been intensely Hebraic rather than classical Greek, if I might employ the distinction first made by Matthew Arnold in the nineteenth century. But I was and have remained a Hebrew rather than a Rabbinic Jew or a passionate Zionist. This might also explain my lifelong affinity for Calvinism, a point that I have often discussed with my friend Jim Kurth, a devout Presbyterian and a distinguished author on foreign relations. Like Jim, I believe in an emphatically judgmental

Deity whose providence is inscrutable to humanity, but which we must try to understand within the limits of our flawed nature. The Bible offers a guideline to the ethical order established by this Deity, and it also depicts His prophets and chosen people acting out the redemptive history that He has shaped with their interaction. Although I continue to be troubled by the harsh judgments visited on ancient idolatrous tribes, the commandment to wipe them out does fit into a larger scheme of *Heilsgeschichte* [redemptive history]. A nation devoted to the one God had to separate itself from its neighbors after it had become aware of itself and its religious mission. The best I can do in trying to treat such behavior charitably, is to view it as a historical stage on the way to a fuller religious consciousness—rather than as a permanent counsel for dealing with those whose ethical and spiritual lives seem defective. Perhaps on this point I am closer to Spinoza, the first religious evolutionary thinker, than I am to either Calvin or the Orthodox Rabbinate. Perhaps, too, it is high time to get back to the narrative that I abandoned a few pages back.

In the end I decided to stay at Yeshiva, and during the last two years there I began to establish some friendships, mostly with other outsiders and with several highly accessible professors. Among these professorial mentors was Maurice Chernowitz, the son of a famous Hebrew scholar and poet from the Crimea. Despite truly dreary teaching assignments, Maurice stayed on at Yeshiva because it was only a short walk from his apartment, and because he was able to supplement his otherwise meager income by moonlighting at several other colleges in the New York area. He was one of the most gifted linguists I have known, and among his accomplishments was to have translated long segments of the work of two of his favorite authors, Schopenhauer and Proust, into modern Hebrew. He had also written a magisterial work, which was published by Harvard, on Proust and the French Impressionists. Whenever I think of my limited rewards as an academician, I try to keep in mind that Maurice, his wife Rose, and their two daughters lived in a cramped apartment on what must have been a shoestring. Until I went to Yale and met Herbert Marcuse, I encountered no one who emitted the same kind of humanistic learning as did this impecunious professor.

In graduate school, I noticed that my classmates hesitated to respond when professors posed questions in class. I'm not sure whether this silence was occasioned by ignorance or by a desire not to be viewed as overly forward. After a few weeks I settled into the same habit as most of my taciturn classmates, although I noticed that when the same students repaired to their study room on the third floor of Yale's Sterling Library they would talk to each other nonstop. They would discourse on the evils of Southern racism and, even more loudly, on the "illegal" war in Vietnam. The discussants could be divided into three distinct cultural-religious groups. The Jews, mostly from New York, raged with anger against the "fascist" war president Lyndon Johnson, but when the Six Days War between Israel and its neighbors erupted, they became a vocal war party. I shall take David Horowitz's word when he says that the Jews whom he knew in the '60s were pro-PLO as well as anti-American, but that was certainly not my experience. A lone exception was a very idealistic Jewish girl who was married to the (very WASP) son of the head of the Canadian Communist Party. This thoroughly sweet young woman seemed crestfallen that her fellow Jews abandoned the leftist party line as soon as the topic turned to Israel.

The Catholics who gathered in the graduate study room were for the most part Irish, and they slavishly followed the Jewish Left on the subjects of Southern bigotry and the Vietnam War. But the Catholic antiwar types seemed far less bellicose than their Jewish classmates when it came to the Arab-Israeli conflict, which they treated as symptomatic of a lack of "international understanding." They also tried to give their then fashionable leftist views a Catholic twist. Thus, they emphasized the fondness expressed by antiwar Democratic Senator Eugene McCarthy for Saint Thomas More, the figure for whom the parish church adjacent to campus had been named. Or else they talked about the need to organize prayer vigils at their local churches against "this unspeakable violence."

Unlike the religious-ethnic minorities, the Protestants tended to belong to the WASP establishment, and they seem to have been thinking about making careers by exploiting what remained of the old-boy network. Politically they were moderate, in the sense of the insipidness that Jesus urged his followers in the Gospels to "spit out." Most of them were "Hugh Scott Republicans," self-described followers of the proverbially centrist Republican senator from the Philadelphia mainline who is best remembered for collecting Ming-dynasty Chinese vases. Their Jewish classmates despised these models of vacuous niceness, who, from their paranoid perspective, would turn against the "minorities" as soon as the occasion presented itself. From my perspective, however, these Protestant classmates, with notable exceptions, foreshadowed the PC types whom I describe in my book *Multiculturalism and the Politics of Guilt* (2002). Those who would later take over elite society's reins from these mannered, torpid types would be far more prejudiced but also more vigorous—and in a certain way they deserved the prize of success.

But there was also a saving remnant of the Protestant students whom I found congenial, and these companions seemed to be as depressed or stunned by the lethargy and opportunism of the WASP majority as I was. Bill Dennis, who for many years worked for Liberty Fund; William Marshner, a thoughtful classicist who would soon convert to the blackest form of ultramontanism; and Dale Van Kley, a future Calvinist historian and theologian, were three of these worthwhile companions to whom I attached myself. Through Marshner and Dennis, I became introduced to a group called the Yale Party of the Right, which held stimulating discussions about political legitimacy and the pitfalls of mass democracy. It was while attending functions of the Party of the Right that I met the *National Review* literary editor Frank Meyer and his son Gene. Through these friendships I later began reviewing books for *National Review*, and when I received an invitation to be interviewed for a job at Rockford College in 1972, it was Frank's widow Elsie who recommended me for the post in a conversation with Rockford provost Gordon Wesner.

Most of my classes, except for my encounter with Herbert Marcuse (the subject of chapter 3), were remarkably uneventful, and I can't say that it made much of a difference for my life or historical perspective that I moved from medieval into modern European history. The medievalist at Yale, Roberto Lopez, was a garden-variety Marxist materialist and Italian anticlerical (supposedly of Spanish Jewish ancestry). Although Lopez's teaching style had a certain Latin spontaneity, his focus on commercial contracts was not exactly what had turned me on about medieval studies in the first place. Since I had studied several European languages beside German, I decided to try my hand at a later European period. The professor I got stuck with, the eminent left-leaning German émigré Hajo Holborn, became the bane of my graduate-school existence because of his idée fixe about hunting for the roots of Nazism in the German past. I did not share this particular passion, and in the end I prepared a dissertation on Catholic romanticism in Central Europe that would not have satisfied my professor's very exacting preconceptions. Holborn was the first of the antifascist, antinational German historians I encountered, and although he was awesomely learned in his field, his conclusions were invariably prescribed. As I explained them to my friends: "the Krauts were always to blame and always leaning toward you know whom." As it became obvious that we were hopelessly at loggerheads, despite the fact that he had previously awarded me honors on my orals, something fateful occurred. Professor Holborn was struck with a debilitating stroke, and I was transferred to a colleague of his, Sidney Ahlstrom, an American religious historian who had just finished directing the dissertation of George Marsden, who was later to become a distinguished scholar of American religion. Ahlstrom was not only open to my arguments but also a gentleman with an unforgettably sweet disposition. The two of us developed a close friendship, and I was grieved when I heard that Sidney—who produced, among other opera, an encyclopedic work on American religious history—had died following the ravages of Alzheimer's disease.

My first job, in the Humanities Division of the University College at Michigan State University, resulted from my failure to listen to the chairman with sufficient attention when he came to interview me during a historical conference in New York. I wrongly gathered the impression that I would be in a high-powered program based on the study of great books from antiquity to the present. What I actually signed on for was teaching MSU undergraduates a watered-down, prepackaged course in Western civ. I was therefore relieved when after a year I could pack my belongings and trudge over to Cleveland, where I had obtained a position as a Europeanist in the Case Western Reserve History Department.

While in East Lansing, Michigan, I made two lifelong contacts, one with Russell Kirk and the other with my future wife Dana. Russell had previously taught in the same department and although he had left with profound dissatisfaction, as I learned from former colleagues, he still lived no more than an hour and a half north of the MSU campus in the hamlet of Mecosta on the sandy pine barrens of Lower Michigan. After having first called, I went to Mecosta to visit Russell, his wife Annette, and their newborn daughter Monica. During the ten months I spent in Michigan, I visited them multiple times; and despite the physical distance of their home from my noisy student apartment in East Lansing, I came to look upon them as close friends in an area that was far from my parents' Connecticut home.

How I met my first wife is a more complex story. Indeed, it was the unforeseen consequence of other events. We met at a wedding in Toronto, in which the groom was my colleague at MSU and the bride a childhood friend of Dana's. The groom intended to "fix me up" with his cousin, who seemed to be a younger version of former New York Congresswoman Bella Abzug. She also came equipped with parents who were utterly stereotypical: the mother was caring but overbearing and the father meek to the point of being nonexistent. My friend helpfully tried to explain that this was "the Jewish side of my family; the other side is Polish." My rhetorical question at the time was, "Do I have to meet them as well?" My future wife was a shy Polish-Canadian with a Jewish father, which in the ethnically insensitive but hypocritically misrepresented Canadian urban society into which she had been thrust put her in a socially awkward situation (to engage in understatement).

Dana was put at the same table where I was sitting. Her father, a courteous Old World gentleman, brought her over while giving her reassurances that she would not feel out of place. Despite the white powder with which she had covered her cheeks and the horned-rim glasses she wore, I noticed that Dana had a beautiful Slavic face. She was also far more composed than my friend's cousin, who made all kinds of unpleasant noises when an announcement was made that we'd soon be "toasting her Majesty the Queen." Of all political attitudes, antimonarchism in the modern age has always struck me as the most bizarre. How can one get annoyed over a middle-aged maternal figurehead symbolizing imperial unity? When I once heard the Straussian political scientist Walter Berns, who was then residing in Toronto, rage against the English monarchy in a lecture, I walked out thinking that I had just heard the ravings of a madman.

A few weeks later I made a second trip to Toronto after having driven my mother to visit her sister in nearby Buffalo, New York. Before leaving for Canada, I called Dana, whom I had told that I would "drop by" whenever I came back, to let her know of my imminent return. Although she was not the only person whom I was planning to see in Toronto, she immediately offered to have me stay with her and her parents in their apartment, which was on the third floor of the old mansion on Palmerston Boulevard (near the University of Toronto) that also housed her father's medical practice. When I arrived, I took an immediate liking not only to the daughter but also to the parents, both of whom had survived with dignity the grim fate of having been overrun by both the Nazis and the Soviets. Each had lost family members to different invaders, and Dana's father had observed that not even his father's great wealth had protected him, his wife, and (probably) his daughter from being shot by the SS. It was harder to figure out what had happened to Dana's mother's family, some of whom had been in the Polish Army. "Either Hitler got them or else they died in a Soviet gulag," Dana matter-of-factly explained.

Although her mother was already suffering from the onset of Alzheimer's, this likeable lady insisted on preparing the evening's meal. The tasty repast featured something like Russian blinis, filled with chopped meat. I ended up spending my entire stay in Toronto at Dana's parents' apartment, and on my next visit I proposed marriage to their only child. She and her parents accepted me, and about a year later we were married. As I reflect on my wife of twenty-five years and her family, I am still shocked to think about how much suffering befell these extraordinarily good people. Dana's parents were separated for eleven years following the war because of my father-in-law's flight from Communist Poland and his subsequent inability to bring his wife and daughter to Canada until 1956; when the family was at last reunited, my mother-in-law came down with Alzheimer's, from which she died soon after my marriage to Dana. Then my wife, who by then was the mother of five children, developed breast cancer in her early forties; despite medical assurances that the cancer was only incipient, she died five years later as a consequence of her illness, just after her father had died from the debilitating effects of a massive stroke. There is now no one left of that wondrous European family that I encountered during my visit to Toronto in 1968. Even the building in which they lived, and the adjacent property that my father-in-law owned and in which the family of David Frum once rented commercial space, no longer stand.

I am inwardly troubled by all the moving I put my wife through because of the uncertain profession I entered. I did not have my contract renewed either at Case Western Reserve or at my next post, New York University, but in neither case was this because of defective scholarship or teaching. Rather, I held the wrong political views—and admitted openly that I had voted for Richard Nixon in 1968. It was not until I obtained my senior professorship at Rockford College in 1973 that my growing family could enjoy the security of staying more than a brief time in a particular place. The thirteen years I spent in Rockford were among my happiest years, even if they were also among my leanest ones as a scholar. Dana and I were full-time, and even doting, parents, although my kids were correct to observe that what I made them do—for example, playing tennis, cross-country skiing, and cycling—were activities that I myself relished. I recently observed to my friend Mark Henrie, when he and his family were visiting, that he was a much more bookish parent than I had been. It was Dana who, like Mark, insisted that the children exert themselves academically. I preferred taking them on bicycle rides or else going ice-skating with Barbara and Joey.

In the summers we would typically take trips, usually heading out West in a rented trailer; once we got as far as the Pacific Ocean, in Oregon. My grandson Joshua has picked up my peculiar habit of exploring maps and driving long distances, a penchant that seems to have skipped an entire generation in my family. One reason that I was so intent on driving west is that as a longtime resident of the Northeast who was born and raised in a European family, I knew zilch about most of the U.S., except for what I saw on TV or read in the papers. Living in what I then (wrongly) believed was the center of our country, it was easier for me to drive through the Western states than it would have been if I had still been in the East. Years later, I would make tortuous car trips with my second wife Mary through the South, a history-drenched region that I did not tour by car until I was almost sixty.

Things began unraveling professionally after I felt constrained to leave Rockford during what turned out to be a financial crisis caused by corrupt leadership. My friend, the Edmund Burke scholar Peter Stanlis, left for the same reason that I did, and as the amount of the embezzlement in which the president was involved became apparent, the college was forced to downsize drastically as well as to replace its top man posthaste. By that time I had taken a position as senior editor at *The World and I* in Washington, D.C. Once there, I became entangled in a messy imbroglio surrounding my proposed appointment at Catholic University of America. It is no longer much of a secret that I intended to use my post at the Washington Times Corporation as a stepping stone to the CUA position, which, I was given reason to believe, would be offered to me as soon as it was authorized. But neoconservatives had other plans, and they were successful in keeping me out of the position even if they could not fill it with one of their own. (Here one thinks of the metaphor of the half-filled glass, for them but not me.)

From there the impetus of our lives pushed us on to Central Pennsylvania, where I had received a senior professorship and, finally, an endowed chair in the humanities at Elizabethtown College. For a few years Dana and I and the younger children (the older ones were already in college) tried to build our social lives in Lancaster, which is still in my opinion one of the most scenic cities—characterized by stately homes and tree-lined streets—in the U.S. We decided to move into a comfortable old neighborhood near Wheaton, the estate of President James Buchanan, and we poured whatever money had been left to us by our deceased parents into expanding a stone-framed house at the edge of the township (which is adjacent to the City of Lancaster). But by then Dana was suffering the effects of what we soon learned was a recurrence of her breast cancer, a condition that we had hoped would not come back but which is invariably fatal when it does. She died after struggling with this hopeless condition for two years, and she remained until the end of her conscious life more concerned about her children than about her debilitated body.

Let me state that in almost every way my present position is better than the one I would have likely found in the contentious environment of CUA, particularly given that university's generally low salaries and the high costs of living in the D.C. area. What made me determined to land that job, however, was the health of my wife and her stated reluctance to move one more time. From what I gather, a persistent charge raised against me at the time of this affair, particularly by one effusively hostile member of the history department, was that I was "not reliable on Israel." This charge was astonishing for two reasons: One, my job, if it had been bestowed on me, would have been to teach ancient political texts, not Middle Eastern politics; and two, to the extent I had expressed any views on Middle Eastern affairs, I had taken the side of the Israelis. The real reason I suspect that my key opponent had attacked me as an anti-Zionist was that my views on the causes of World War I did not mesh with those of his anti-German émigré professor at Columbia. This opponent had previously expressed horror that I had dared to criticize his mentor in print.

It was while dealing with grieving children, the loss of my first wife, and a house that cost more than I could afford that I met my present wife Mary. She is right to describe herself as a "problem-solver." When she stepped into my unbearably complicated life as a widower a bit over thirteen years ago, she knew she was asking for trouble. I had met her several years earlier, when I was still new to Elizabethtown. Mary would sit in the corner of the Jay's Nest, which was something between a student meeting place and a short-order culinary alternative to the regular dining facilities, reading a book during her lunch hours. She appeared to be a sweet, demure soul who, although then a book manager in the college store, avoided unnecessary social contact with her customers. My Elizabethtown colleague Wes McDonald informed me that she had once been "some kind of hippie," and she and her husband, who had been a Marine during the Vietnam War, were building a "house that still had no running water." In fact, Mary's life was far more complicated than Wes's description suggested. The person she had been married to for almost twenty years was a highly talented craftsman and a Pennsylvania Dutch local. Despite a generally kindly disposition, however, his war experiences had taken their toll; and his attempts to "build a log cabin in the woods" on land they had purchased was interrupted by the effects of posttraumatic stress. I was not surprised, therefore, when a few years later Mary and this husband agreed to an amicable parting. Although their union had been for Mary exceedingly difficult, to this day she regrets that her earlier marriage did not work out.

After Dana died, and about a year after Mary's divorce, I began to see Mary as being more than someone I occasionally encountered in the college store. Despite her difficulties in winning acceptance from my children, who had been devastated by their mother's unexpected cancer recurrence and eventual passing, Mary persisted in her very shy way until she had gained their confidence. We married several years later, after I had moved from my high-maintenance dwelling in Lancaster to our present brick abode, flanked by magnolia trees, across from the admissions office of Elizabethtown College.

Mary has been justified in taking credit for two achievements since knowing me. One has been to look after my demanding youngest daughter, whom Mary spent several vexing years trying to help through adolescence. Mary, my eldest daughter, and my son-in-law all contributed to this often thankless task. Her other achievement has been to encourage me to start writing books again, for I had lost creative steam following a series of family deaths and professional setbacks. Although our tastes and interests often diverge, Mary was a major force in getting me to finish my last four books. During conversations, moreover, she provided the catchy subtitles for *Multiculturalism and the Politics of Guilt: Toward a Secular Theocracy* and *Conservatism in America: Making Sense of the American Right*. The original title for the latter book, "Baseless Conservatism," was also Mary's, but the publisher opted for the more pedestrian one it ultimately received.

I would be remiss if I concluded this section without addressing a charge that has been leveled against me, and most hurtfully, by a well-known political theorist during my hardships at CUA. I am allegedly a "controversialist and not a scholar," and my reputation has been built on quarreling with neoconservative journalists. There are two responses to be made here. One, the bulk of my published books and most of my long articles concern scholarly subjects, ranging from ancient historiography to European intellectual history, as well as studies of various political movements. My trilogy on the democratic administrative state and its changing ideologies of control deal only parenthetically with neoconservatism. While the neoconservative and liberal establishments unfairly depict my work as extremist attacks on their positions, they have never made clear in what way my views are "extreme."

My critical references to neoconservative journalists, moreover, are often made in the context of examining the post-Marxist Left and its cultural effects. Admittedly I have balked at the idea of recognizing the neoconservatives as part of any conceivable Right; nonetheless, this is not based on a lack of charity. The reason for my judgment is that these people have struck me as paradigmatic leftists who are counterfactually identified as "conservatives." While this interpretation may mystify country-club Republicans and neo-Wilsonian global democrats, it makes perfectly good sense to the young European scholars with whom I have been in contact. Academics in Eastern Europe are particularly open to my ideas, and for an obvious reason: They come from regions that have not undergone the kind of intense media and educational socialization that has been the fate of Western "liberal democracies" since the 1960s.

Multiculturalism and the Politics of Guilt and *The Strange Death of Marxism* (2005) are both available in several foreign languages, including Russian, and each is selling better in Europe than it is in the U.S. Despite neglect in the American national press, *The Strange Death of Marxism* has received considerable attention in Polish, Spanish, and Russian newspapers, and it was the subject of a long, favorable review in the leading "conservative" Athenian daily, *Hellenikes Grammes*. *Multiculturalism* in German translation was honored in the *Frankfurter Allgemeine Zeitung* as one of the year's best books in 2005. Sometimes I imagine how well my work might sell in my own country if only my adversaries were not around.

My attitude toward the neoconservatives was not always hostile. In the early 1970s I had been drawn to some of them as critics of the counterculture, and I persisted in reading *Commentary* with some regularity until the mid-1980s. But by the late 1970s I noticed with growing discomfort the unalterably leftist sensibilities of many neoconservative journalists and social scientists. Most troubling of all, they did not fundamentally change their direction, which is the conventional view, but rather moved in the opposite direction the more firmly they came to control the conservative movement. In *Conservatism in America*, I try to document the misleading way in which this reality has been depicted. On race issues, McCarthyism, and gay activism, neoconservatives in the 1970s stood well to the right of where they would later drag the "conservative movement."

As I reflected in the late 1970s on such characteristic views of theirs as attachment to the anti-Soviet Left, a fixation on Christian anti-Semitism, and a raging hatred of Germans, Russians, and white Southerners, it dawned on me that I was looking at a mere variation on those usual opinions that could be found in the *New York Review of Books* or *New Republic*. What distinguished the neoconservatives from their establishment Left dinner companions, however, were two areas of disagreement: a differing level of concern about Israel, and an obvious annoyance with blacks over anti-Semitic incidents that had erupted in New York during the early 1970s. But one should not exaggerate either difference. It was the neoconservatives' unbroken good relations with the liberals, for whose publications they continued to write, which was their trump card in competing for control over the conservative establishment. My noticing of such details did not render me a jaundiced commentator on the rise of the neoconservatives to power. It left me a more acute observer of what others chose to ignore. And while the offended partisans reacted by striking back at me, this had no effect on how I perceived their worldview. I had written about neoconservatives and their mindset critically as early as 1983, in an essay published in *Modern Age*. That essay had drawn on material I had been assembling since the 1970s, well before my differences with neoconservative journalists had put me in harm's way.

There is one widespread criticism of the neoconservatives that I have never accepted. Contrary to the opinion of some of their adversaries, it does not seem to me that the neoconservatives' Zionist loyalties and support for the nationalist Right in Israel provide an all-purpose key for grasping their ideological universe. When I encountered Taki's characterization of *Commentary* as the "Likud Party's mouthpiece," I found myself thinking: "Were that all the magazine did, front for the Israeli Right!" One does not have to embrace the entire package of neoconservative positions in order to be for the Israeli government or against its Palestinian foes. One could conceivably sympathize with the Southern side in the U.S. Civil War, lean toward the Central Powers in the First World War, or believe that Martin Luther King was not a secular saint but a

Marxist demagogue and still be passionately supportive of Israel, as I explained in a feature essay on the changing foreign policy of the American Right in *Orbis* (Winter 2007). Not every part of the neoconservative bundle of sentiments is related to every other one; nor does it receive its motive power exclusively from the impulse to rally to the Israeli government against its critics.

Jim Kurth, an international-relations expert, has often defended the Israelis against the Palestinians, but there is little else of a political or historical nature on which Jim and the neoconservatives would agree. The neoconservative belief cluster, much of which has been imposed on "conservative" foundations and publications, cannot be reduced to the one position of unconditional support for the Israeli Right. At the heart of that body of beliefs and feelings is a leftist vision of the world, one in which historical nations are replaced by aggregations of individuals held together by a shared belief in equality and "human rights." Although a Jewish exception to this rule is characteristic of neoconservative discourse, even the Israelis are presented counterfactually not as a historic nation but as a Middle Eastern adjunct to the global democratic enterprise.

The neoconservative vision of "propositional nations" is a constructivist project that resembles the noteworthy efforts by German antinationalist Jürgen Habermas to create for his country a "constitutional patriotism." This Habermasian alternative to real national identity was intended to function as a public philosophy for Germans after the disgrace of the Nazi regime. In this scheme, which has become public and educational policy in Germany, one does not have to deal with flesh-and-blood people invested with inherited identities that are worth preserving. For the Germans, such a move could never be allowed because it would allegedly bring with it a renewed danger of "German fascism." The neoconservatives have produced their own milder equivalent of the Habermasian project. Both their enthusiasm for Third World immigration and their opposition to immigration restrictionists flow from their view that populations are interchangeable. All people are "individuals" who can be socialized in the same way, providing they are molded by a suitable public administration and by a steady diet of human-rights talk. Because, like the earlier Progressives, the neoconservatives associate public education with "democratic patriotism," and because they link morality to "democratic values," they have been allowed to appropriate for themselves the "conservative" mantle. This, in my opinion, is a case of mistaken identity.

Like the post-Marxist Left in Europe, the neoconservatives find positive merit in consumer capitalism, especially if it helps to break down national and regional barriers and to homogenize different cultures. For this procapitalist stance neoconservatives are praised in the Republican press as "moderates" and critics of state socialism. Another characteristic neoconservative view is that Americans are a "right-of-center people": by which is meant that while we accept spousal unions and minority set-asides, we have been more reluctant than Europeans to tax productive citizens punitively. It might be asked whether those who favor such positions are in any meaningful sense "conservatives"—or something other than leftists who have replaced state socialism with social engineering. My understanding of neoconservatives, it might be argued, is insufficiently generous or insufficiently nuanced, but if that is the case I would like to hear the neoconservatives' response. Until now they have not replied to me, except by treating me as a liar or a lunatic.

My second response to the charge that I am a "controversialist" is that I never intended to trade scholarly activities for a career of political polemics. That is how my life worked out, because the establishment Left and, later, the neoconservatives managed to keep me from obtaining desirable academic positions. The neoconservatives have been equally diligent in turning my academic exertions into exercises in futility. When my scholarly work *After Liberalism* (1999) came out in a prestigious Princeton University Press series, it was not reviewed in any publication over which the neoconservatives exerted even minimal influence. The *New Republic* did break ranks here, and it might have been the only non-paleoconservative publication that gave my book a respectful hearing, thanks to the maverick leftist reviewer Alan Wolfe. Incidentally: one would have had to search with a fine-tooth comb to locate anything in this study, which dealt with the "liberal idea" and public administration since the nineteenth century, that could be read as an explicit attack on the neoconservative worldview. But my failure to recognize this persuasion as the true heir of the liberal tradition might have caused negative reactions among those few neoconservatives who bothered to read my book.

    I have always tried to avoid confrontation in my social and personal life. Mary is wont to refer to me as "the marshmallow" because of my tendency to make excessive concessions to my children and students, a practice that is derived from my instinctive repugnance for conflict. It took considerable provocation to turn me into the attack dog I eventually became in dealing with the neoconservatives and their work. And even in playing this adversarial role, I have tried to limit my editorializing and certainly any personal contact with my opponents. It is hard for me emotionally to debate neoconservatives or their dependents, in the same way that it is obviously unacceptable for them to be around me. And as a senior citizen, I look forward to the time when others who are younger and healthier can remove the critical burden from my shoulders. For me it is more gratifying to study Polybius and Hegel than to tackle the windy, bellicose prose of Norman Podhoretz and Michael Ledeen. Recently, I surprised an editor of *Modern Age* who, when he asked me for a feature essay on interwar Habsburg conservatism, got exactly what he requested. He seemed displeased that I had submitted what were close textual readings rather than a sample of my "explosive prose." The point I made at that time is that I prefer writing the first to producing the second. If the neoconservatives and others on the left had not undermined my career decades ago, that might have been just about the only kind of work I would have produced.

A certain distinction should be drawn nonetheless between what are intended to be polemics and more analytic discussions of neoconservatism and the traditions on which it builds. Let me come back to a point suggested earlier. Underlining a relation between what Mark Gerson has called the "neoconservative vision" and various leftist ideologies does not constitute a putdown. It is an attempt to clarify a political genealogy. No matter what neoconservative journalists may think about critical discussions of their worldview, such a practice should not be equated with hurling insults.

The study of modern ideology as a peculiarly leftist phenomenon has interested me since the 1960s, and it is easy to trace a thematic line from my first book, on romantic millenarianism, through my trilogy on the ideologies of the democratic managerial state, down to my recent monograph on the transformations of the American Right. They all engage such broad intertwining topics as apocalyptic religion, the Enlightenment notion of Progress, and the evolution of the democratic Left. Needless to say, this research focus entered my work long before my unhappy encounter with the neoconservatives, but when I did encounter them, they seemed to exemplify much of what I had been writing about. A young Polish scholar, Juliusz Jablecki, has brought to my attention how closely the neoconservatives' favored global democratic order resembles the expressed ideals of the Polish Jewish political activist Adam Michnik. Like his American counterparts, Michnik, whose parents were Stalinists in postwar Poland, broke from Marxist-Leninism because it was supposedly anti-Semitic and politically reactionary. Michnik points to the German antifascist leftist Jürgen Habermas as a proper guide for Poland's path toward "multicultural democracy." Jablecki treats Michnik and the American neoconservatives as equally paradigmatic of what I have called the "post-Marxist Left," although he sees this Left as now engaged in combat with a more radical Left, which is both anti-Zionist and pro-Muslim.

Although my young Polish friend may say things that do not please the *Commentary* editorial board, what he is pursuing is a scholarly exercise. He is looking for forms of unrecognized leftist thinking in the current political climate. And as a researcher, he does not have to be impressed by the fact that some post-Marxist leftists have become without theoretical justification the establishment Right. This media whim has no more necessary relevance for the pursuit of intellectual history than if the *New York Times* decided to describe Joseph Stalin as a monarchist or Hillary Clinton as a traditional Christian homemaker. The refusal to call neoconservatives what we are supposed to call them may be politically and professionally imprudent. But it is not a factual error; nor is the practice of raising troublesome genealogical questions about the "neoconservative vision" a less than honorable endeavor for a student of modern ideologies.

RICHARD NIXON

March 23, 1990

577 CHESTNUT RIDGE ROAD
WOODCLIFF LAKE, NEW JERSEY

Dear Paul,

I want you to know how thoroughly I enjoyed your piece on Disraeli. You will not be surprised to learn that I totally agree with your appraisal of him.

Contrary to the public impression, I was never under the illusion that Disraeli was a closet liberal. He was, in fact, a brilliant practical politician whose heart was not with the working class voters he enfranchised, but with the land owning Tories whose approval he craved.

Incidentally, I have always thought that he was wrong and that Peel was right on the repeal of the Corn Laws.

With warm regards,

Sincerely,

Dr. Paul Gottfried

III

The Marcuse Factor

One experience that left its mark on me as a graduate student at Yale University came in the spring of 1964, when Herbert Marcuse (1898–1979) arrived to teach a course in the history of socialism. With his flowing gray hair, aquiline nose, imposingly long figure, and distinguished German accent, Marcuse became for me a role model. It may be necessary to explain the reasons for this attraction. Certainly our political views were not the same. While I proudly belonged to the Yale Party of the Right (despite my identification as a Rockefeller Republican), Marcuse had supported the Soviet suppression of the Hungarian uprising in 1956. He also lavished praise on Castro and other Communist despots and held no brief for Western bourgeois society, or what remained of it. Most annoyingly, he referred to those who were left-of-center in American politics as reactionaries and treated the welfare state as an instrument for desensitizing American consumers to the evils of capitalism.

Despite these quirks, our new professor was a dazzling lecturer. He knew about subjects that at the time gripped me keenly: European intellectual history and especially German philosophy. I had grown up knowing German, and I had dipped into Kant, Hegel, and Schopenhauer years before enrolling in Marcuse's course. He brought up German philosophers and other thinkers, like Pascal, Maistre, and Proudhon, while quoting long passages in the original languages, and he blew me away as an intellectually curious twenty-three-year-old auditor in his class. What is more, his background reminded me of my father's family, German-speaking Jews who had fled from the Nazis and spoke English with a similar inflection. At the time I knew Marcuse, he had not yet become the gray eminence of the New Left. He was still a philosophy professor at Brandeis University who took a train to New Haven once a week to hold a class at the Yale Graduate Hall. It was only later, when he had retired from Brandeis and had gone to San Diego State as a teacher, that he went off the deep end. In his California phase he openly advocated violence and became identified with the black Communist Party activist Angela Davis. Thirty years later, when I spoke to Hegel scholar Stanley Rosen about his one meeting with Marcuse, Rosen remembered the person whom I had known—a charming Old World academic with a touch of dottiness. Rosen, too, was stunned by what Marcuse did in California. He attributed such behavior to the lack of a moral center, a problem that Rosen had explored in a critical study of Martin Heidegger.

As a student I had perceived such a problem, but I had also found ways of rationalizing it by turning Marcuse's flaws into signs of virtue. His outbursts against capitalist one-dimensionality and his corresponding indulgence of Communist mass murder were attributable to his *ancien régime* elegance and to his genuine shock over American consumerist habits. For the most part, however, I tried not to think about his wicked opinions, because there was no possibility of reconciling them with my fierce anticommunism. Even less did I care for the fantasy that Marcuse had inserted into *Eros and Civilization* (1955): that a fusion of Marx and Freud would take place in a future socialist world practicing polymorphic sexuality. Although these grotesque themes turned up in his contributions to German journals of the 1930s, Marcuse's erotic fixation was not what drew me to him philosophically or socially. Given my uptight Central European bourgeois upbringing, I could not envisage the forbidden pleasures that Marcuse hoped to make available by slaying the capitalist monster. And though he had published a thick volume on Soviet communism in 1958 that was sympathetically critical of his subject, it was hard for me to imagine that he or anyone else believed that Stalin was enabling his Russian subjects to enjoy sensual pleasures. Or that the Soviets were featuring more of such pleasures than "repressed" consumers could pick up in Times Square. As I later figured out, Marcuse leaned toward the Soviets for the same reason that he conceived of Western capitalist countries as sexually repressive. Like other members of the Frankfurt School, and especially Theodor Adorno, with whom he had been hanging out in the early '30s, Marcuse claimed to detest bourgeois civilization and wished to see it destroyed.

Still and all, his connection to what he professed to despise was ambivalent and, like other members of the Frankfurt School, as noted by Lorenz Jäger in his biography of Adorno, Marcuse was in some ways a bourgeois anachronism. This was evident from the way he dressed to the gallant (but never lecherous) manner in which he spoke to female students. With his extensive humanistic and linguistic erudition, he oozed traditional German *Bildung*, a quality that contrasted sharply with the careerism and narrow specialization that I had encountered among most of my American professors.

Marcuse was also unconcerned about the kinds of issues that filled the political agendas of my left-of-center classmates. At my graduation ceremony at Yeshiva University in June 1963, our invited speaker was Justice Arthur Goldberg, who proudly pointed to his record in ordering the desegregation of public schools in the American South. Some of my classmates went agog over what Goldberg said not only because he was Jewish and from New York but also because they were apparently deeply concerned about court-ordered desegregation in Southern counties, places that none of us had ever visited and barely knew existed. At the time I could not figure out why adolescents who rarely spoke to non-Jews and whose only connection to black people came when they purchased subway tokens were so exercised over segregated schools somewhere in North Carolina. These students had never attended public schools even in their predominantly Jewish neighborhoods; almost all of them had gone to private religious academies that drew their students and teachers from very narrow subethnic communities. Years later I felt a comparable degree of astonishment when a Hindu physics professor at Rockford College told me that he would not vote for Ronald Reagan because this Republican presidential candidate had not supported the Equal Rights Amendment. Such an attitude was not at all inconsistent, in this person's mind, with having his wife and daughters walk behind him with bowed heads. Although the ancient Pharisees and Saint Paul might have approved of this Hindu practice, none of them, in contrast to the Indian physics professor, would have likely voted against someone for not supporting the Equal Rights Amendment.

Marcuse not only did not engage in such curious applications of a double standard but also seemed bored by what excited his progressive-minded auditors. Once when a young radical who later found employment at Cornell, Robert Klein, explained to Marcuse that "as a Marxist, I cannot support violence," our teacher looked at him as if he were daft. Another time a young pretty woman from Tennessee whose mother belonged to the state Planned Parenthood League, Eve Pittorelli (her husband was a politically indifferent architect from an immigrant Italian household), noted that our famous leftist mentor exhibited no discernible interest in "women's issues." This was stated a few months before the events leading up to the Supreme Court's decision in *Griswold v. Connecticut,* a case that had been conveniently arranged for the courts when the Planned Parenthood League of Connecticut opened up a center about a stone's throw from where I bought books at the Yale Co-op. The campus was already abuzz with sudden, growing concern about reproductive rights, and I learned from my classmates that it was an "outrage" that contraception was illegal in Connecticut. Until listening to such invective, I had had no idea that such a prohibition existed in the Nutmeg State. Somehow the families in Bridgeport, including the devoutly Catholic Irish ones, had managed to limit the number of their offspring. Perhaps my classmates, even the very geeky ones, had been more sexually active than I was, but it seemed to me silly that people should be running around worrying about a prohibition that had been for the most part applied sporadically and ineffectively.

I suspect that Professor Marcuse, although a notorious womanizer, was even less interested in this archaic, toothless prohibition than I was. He was also far more tolerant of dissenting opinions from his students than were my other professors. When I had criticized Woodrow Wilson and his messianic politics in one of my other classes, the instructor had reacted with extreme displeasure. I felt forced to cut off my remarks lest I injure my professional future by expressing unseasonable views (something that I ultimately did). In Marcuse's class, it was different. Unlike my Cold War liberal professors and current PC colleagues, this graying German radical thrived on debate. When he asked to have a student argue against Karl Marx's interpretation of the Paris uprising of May 1848, an event that was then seen as an early expression of French working-class consciousness, I readily volunteered. My presentation, which I drew for the most part from Alexis de Tocqueville's recollections, brought forth a powerful reaction from my Marxist adversary. But as soon as the give-and-take was over, Marcuse thanked me for my "valorous efforts" and, perhaps to underline his magnanimity, gave me the highest grade for the course. I was put in mind of his generous spirit many times afterwards, and I am still embarrassed to admit that I learned true liberal intellectual exchange from a declared Marxist-Leninist.

Leftist émigré social historians have been partly right to stress the rejection experienced by German Jewish bourgeois in the early twentieth century in an Austro-German society that viewed them mostly as outsiders. Although Jews in Germany succeeded in advancing in the professions and even politics at a much higher rate than elsewhere, possibly including the U.S., there was nonetheless an anti-Semitic legacy that made German Jews despair about their full acceptance into the broader society, even before the Nazis came to power.

Some educated, wealthy German Jews turned toward the cultural and aesthetic Right, as exemplified by the rarefied circle centered around the poet-seer Stefan George. Despite George's reactionary positions, illustrated by his contempt for modernity and his invocation of a "Third Reich" led by spiritual ascetics and artistic purifiers, well over half of his inner circle was Jewish. A German literary commentator, Geret Luhr, has shown in *Ästhetische Kritik der Moderne* (2002) that George's Jewish disciples spanned the political spectrum, from culturally conservative Teutonophile Friedrich Gundolf to Zionist Eric Kahler to Marxist Walter Benjamin. What united the group was an experience of estrangement. They did not fit into their parents' commercial world any better than they did into a German society that continued to keep them at arm's length. One is struck by the frequency with which such souls contemplated and in some cases committed suicide. George incarnated, albeit for different reasons, a similar alienation and happily accepted the flatteries of young Jews, even suggesting in an oft-quoted poem in *Stern des Bundes* (1913) that he was mediating artistically between "the swarthy and blond brothers who had sprung from the same womb but who do not recognize each other, and therefore wander forever, without being fulfilled." (The reader is asked to put up with this translation of a difficult, brilliant poet. Had I been alive at that time, I too in all likelihood would have been a *George-Anhänger*.)

But another reaction that arose among snubbed German Jewish bourgeois was an antinational, antibourgeois stance that easily morphed into reckless social radicalism. While the forms taken by this reaction have not always been particularly salutary, for many years I had hoped to separate the fruits from their bitter source. In my former view, those who had tried to expose the corruptness and oppressive condition of pre-socialist Western life were exaggerating middle-class, capitalist malevolence because of the circumstances of their youth and because of their perpetual search for a "fascist" enemy after their experience with the Nazis. Nonetheless, I persisted in thinking that it was possible to extract from this trauma a core of methodological truth. Despite their derailments, Marcuse and his friends did carry with them a usable form of social analysis, a philosophy of history, and an awareness of the ideological dimension of political life, all of which Anglo-American society was ignoring or obdurately refused to incorporate into its self-studies. I arrived at this view after having studied under Marcuse as a rapt, indulgent disciple, and after having come to respect his learning.

I was outraged that the Yale graduate school would not offer him a chair in the history of socialism and Marxism after his expected retirement from Brandeis. Having voted in the fall (reluctantly) for

Goldwater as president, I found it hypocritical to condemn my professors for right-wing bigotry. But when a classmate began to condemn the anti-Marcuseites as "liberal fascists," I decided to adopt that term. I could thereby attack my professors, who were mostly Kennedy-Johnson Democrats, without having to move leftward and while continuing to support my teacher, who by then was heading west. What might have put him over the edge on the West Coast, I long believed, were the unwillingness of Brandeis to extend his contract (beyond the retirement age) and the refusal of Yale to establish a position for a distinguished visiting professor. When Marcuse on a visit to Venice told the mayor that there were too many tasteless visitors there, and that "si ha bisogno qua d'un turismo di qualità" (one needs a tourism of a high quality), I was actually amused by his remarks. Just because Marcuse was squishy soft on the Commies, I thought, did not require him to accept the improper use of architectural treasures. In any case, he was correct to point out the need to save the physical legacy of the Italian Renaissance from littering tourists.

The last time I came to Marcuse's defense was in 1979, just after his death, when *National Review* published an abrasive obituary. I submitted to the magazine an impassioned retort, noting Marcuse's contribution to Hegel studies in *Reason and Revolution* (1941). NR never published this qualified endorsement of a famous radical. Given my known politics, my gesture might have created cognitive dissonance, even more than the lifelong tendency of Sidney Hook, a fiercely anticommunist social democrat, to talk up Marx. By then I was already to the right of Hook politically, while Marcuse and the Frankfurt School were far more radical, at least culturally, than the Victorian father of communism.

My interest in Marcuse led me to read Adorno and Adorno's collaborator Max Horkheimer, and by the late '80s I became associated with *Telos,* a journal that had been founded to popularize in the U.S. the critical theory of the Frankfurt School, a center of social thought founded in interwar Germany by self-styled social radicals influenced by both Marx and Freud. Under its independent-minded editor-in-chief Paul Piccone, *Telos* had moved generally rightward from its New Leftist beginnings in the '60s; nonetheless, my colleague Wes McDonald expressed horror that I had taken up with these "weird people" who would have looked out of place at an Intercollegiate Studies Institute (ISI) seminar. Despite Wes's objections, I felt *en famille* in my new company, and as my neoconservative adversaries took over leadership positions on the American Right, I felt fully justified in shifting camps. My new comrades were graying New Leftists who had moved by stages away from their originally leftist Frankfurt School positions. By then they were supplementing their changing belief systems or investigative methodologies by adding ideas taken from Carl Schmitt and other European critics of liberalism. In the magazine's issues, one learnt how catastrophically the Communist god had failed, albeit not in the same dramatic fashion as that story unfolds in the book of that title. But I soon offended my new friends. Although they claimed to be looking for ideas, even in the humanism of Irving Babbitt, they always tried to relate whatever they chanced upon to something said by Adorno or by one of his associates in interwar Frankfurt.

By the early '90s I had tired of this cult and of the mechanical hero worship it engendered. Admittedly there were Frankfurt School texts I found instructive, particularly *Dialectic of Enlightenment* (1972) by Adorno and Horkheimer and Adorno's *Negative Dialectics* (1973), both of which analyze social and cultural phenomena in a manner that I as a nonleftist could appreciate. Adorno's attacks on bureaucratic structures and on Enlightenment rationalism, a theme that runs through *Dialectic of Enlightenment*, have profoundly conservative implications, providing that one can separate such perceptions from the muddled syntax in which they are encased. I thought that one should be free to take from Adorno, Horkheimer, and Marcuse what seems relevant, while being permitted to dump the rest. In any case, one should not hesitate to criticize those unsightly defects that marred their interpretive tradition. Not everything that came out of their activity was usable or admirable.

Those opinions, however, did not prevail in the *Telos* circle. Thus, a work as long and influential as *The Authoritarian Personality* (1950), which Adorno, Horkheimer, and other Frankfurt School members constructed during and after the Second World War, was blithely removed from the canon. According to the received doctrine, its purpose was to generate cash for the exiled authors, and its calls for a PC therapeutic regime, I was told, had nothing to do with real Frankfurt School scholarship. Adorno's obsession with "fascist personalities" and his fevered attempt to uncover them among white Christian heterosexuals in the U.S. was supposedly only a wartime aberration.

But even a cursory reading of Rolf Wiggershaus's authoritative German study of the Frankfurt School proves the opposite—namely, that one finds similar recriminatory work done by the usual suspects well before the publication of *The Authoritarian Personality*, going back to Frankfurt in the 1930s. There is also evidence that Adorno rode the same antibourgeois hobbyhorse after his return to Germany in 1950. But it was impossible to discuss any of this with my collaborators without causing noisy, offended denials.

It was also difficult to present to my usually amiable colleagues in New York the (to me) self-evident truth that much of the radical project of the Frankfurt School was attributable to the Jewishness of its founders. Without their sense of marginalization and the attendant hostilities, they would not likely have been so contemptuous of ordinary, non-maladjusted bourgeois. This was particularly true of Adorno, despite his Catholic upbringing and his French mother, whose maiden name he took, and despite the fact that his Jewish father shared none of his hang-ups. A Hungarian Jewish social theorist and onetime *Telos* contributor, Zoltan Tar, had made the same point in exhaustive detail. In *Foundations of the Frankfurt School of Social Research*, Tar had argued that one could not separate Frankfurt School theory from Jewish anxieties. The author documented his plausible contentions with great thoroughness; my friends, however, condemned "his ridiculous nonsense," and they scolded me for taking it seriously.

When I defended Tar's interpretation in an essay for the journal, they became even more visibly annoyed. According to the collective editorial judgment, I was recycling a position that is intrinsically anti-Semitic. The inconsistency in this negative opinion was for me as maddening as the selective victimology practiced by Euro-American multiculturalists. How could one pretend to be looking at the social and existential ground of a political position but then refuse to apply this method to one's own group or mentors? No matter what they claimed about themselves as "free-floating intellectuals" [*freischwebende intelligenz*], members of the Frankfurt School were as influenced by their backgrounds and the baggage it brought as those whom they chose to excoriate.

It was my deepening friendship with Piccone, who died in 2004, and his faithful companion Gary Ulmen, the onetime assistant of anthropologist Karl Wittfogel, which kept me in the *Telos* circle long after my fondness for the Frankfurt School had begun to wane. Piccone, Ulmen, the political theorist George Schwab, and I became fast friends and coworkers on various projects centered on Carl Schmitt. My interest in Schmitt superseded my predilection for critical theory; nonetheless, since the two interests prevailed among the same group and publication, I did not change my circle as much as I did my thinking. I no longer felt compelled to "salvage" anything from the Frankfurt School or to pass it on to a younger generation. The magazine did feature themes that questioned the relevance of critical theory in a self-liquidating bourgeois society; at the same time, most of the contributors clung stubbornly to the old faith even while denying that they did. When the political uses of critical theory seemed to be exhausted, some of my fellow editors took to writing about Adorno's defense and composition of atonal music as a revolt against bourgeois conformity.

By then I was moving even further out of the loop, for I found Adorno's musical compositions to be unfit for human consumption. Would that everyone practiced fascist conformity by emulating Mozart and Vivaldi! Indeed, trying to preserve a living critical theory was coming to resemble the play-acting of contemporary European Marxism. Yuppies in France and Germany who indulge in every PC fad pretend to be Marxists broadly understood. By carefully cherry picking Marx's collected works, they can depict a master who is forever fashionable, whether as an ecologist, an advocate of open borders, or someone who would have championed gay marriage. Among my liberal Christian colleagues the same positions are attributed to Jesus by reducing the New Testament to two or three overworked or deconstructed verses. An honest disciple would abandon a master whose teachings he could no longer accept rather than twist his words into pretzels.

Much has happened to me and to others since I first entered Herbert Marcuse's class. My teacher died after his less than dignified golden years, and my colleagues from *Telos* have either passed on into the *molestam senectutis* or into that which waits us at the end of this aging process. To think of myself now as a disciple of Marcuse or of the broader Frankfurt School movement to which he belonged has become difficult but not impossible. I remain a *Telos* editor, and following the tragic death of our ebullient chief editor, we have continued to meet once a year in mid-January under the auspices of Paul's gracious widow to discuss the publication's future. (It has already been decided that it will continue.) In provocative reviews of my last two books, the analytic philosopher David Gordon has portrayed me as a right-wing exponent of the Frankfurt School. I am what Adorno or Marcuse would have been if they had been bourgeois conservatives, applying their critical method to leftist targets.

This image amuses me, but it overlooks certain elementary distinctions that David understands better than I. You cannot be a critical theorist unless you share the corresponding worldview. A social analyst may adapt Adorno or the Italian Marxist Antonio Gramsci while pursuing diametrically opposed moral and cultural ends. But the effect is not to replicate the same body of thought while transposing it to a different ideological location. To provide a case in point: a right-winger may notice the applicability of critical method for exposing leftist power structures. But the result of applying it is not what the social theorists who fashioned this method intended it to do. There is an intention in political theory, unlike, say, technology, that is inseparable from a particular form of inquiry. No one in his right mind would confuse "right-wing Gramscians," who emphasize the hegemonic ideologies of the left, with the dominant ideas of the Italian Communist Party, which also idolized Gramsci. Context counts in examining the relation of social and political thinkers to each other. And no matter how respectfully men of the right, like the late Sam Francis or Alain de Benoist, have spoken about Gramsci as a methodological teacher, there is a difference between an adaptable idea and the political persuasion to which it pertains.

I make this point in order to emphasize my reservations about describing myself as an Adornoite or Marcuseite simply because I have borrowed from the interwar Left a particular strategy for unmasking contemporary leftists or antitraditional apparatuses of power. Such borrowing is different from membership in the tradition whose ideas one is adapting. For example, those Federalists who framed the Judiciary Act of 1789 were not the precursors of today's judicial activists, even though both favored a powerful judiciary that controlled state legislatures. One group of judicial activists was trying to hold back mass democracy; the other group wishes to push the egalitarian project in a more radical direction than legislatures are likely to go. Intention is integral to our understanding of social and political positions.

What might be argued, however, is that intellectual traditions bind people who otherwise would be separated politically and historically. The French political philosopher Pierre Manent, in his widely read anthology of liberal theorists and in his even better-known *Histoire Intellectuelle du Libéralisme* (1987), links figures who would not likely have agreed on the best form of government but who collectively contributed to a liberal tradition of thought. While Machiavelli, Rousseau, Hobbes, and Montesquieu would not have all rallied to popular government or to the ideal of social equality, according to Manent, they nonetheless represented the developmental stages of a coherent and identifiably liberal worldview. One encounters in their work themes or undercurrents—such as the disentanglement of political life from ecclesiastical authority, a constructivist notion of government, a human nature identified with the individual will's invention of what human beings are, and a separation of state and society—which define a "liberal" postmedieval school of thought. Without embracing his intellectualist approach entirely, it seems to me that Manent is correct to underscore the possibility of a far-ranging agreement about certain premises among thinkers who would not otherwise have had much in common. Thus, he treats side-by-side Montesquieu and Rousseau because of their shared views about the artificiality of government, the association of commercial life with a softening of manners, and a general skepticism about Christianity. This same approach might also indicate that right-wing and left-wing critical theorists hold common assumptions, e.g., about the determinative character of class and history and about the centrality of power in the promotion of modern ideologies.

To whatever extent this exegesis works, I have imitated my teacher Marcuse in the way I have examined particular "values." In the war between the exponents of Nature and History, I generally side with those who stress historical contexts and power relations. Marcuse is not the only thinker who has espoused this perspective, but for me he played a key role in interpreting it. That I later discovered or rediscovered such a perspective in traditionalist and even counterrevolutionary writers is not surprising. By then I was also turning sharply against Marcuse's political teachings and exhibitionism, and (perhaps) I was trying to find other exponents for ideas that I had picked up from him.

There may, however, be something more to this genealogical exploration than my encounter with Marcuse would suggest. About the time I was taking his class, I began reading other authors who became critical for my later thinking. Two texts Marcuse brought up in class and led me to read were Maistre's *Soirées* (1821) and Hegel's *Philosophy of Right* (1821). The attempts by both of these authors, one a Catholic counterrevolutionary and the other a German Protestant monarchist, to understand the impact of history on human nature impressed me deeply as a young man. Not until I read Maistre and Hegel did I reach for Burke's *Reflections* (1790), a tract that I still find compelling as a presentation of historically-based conservatism. Burke's perceptions about the moral value of habituation, the social, hierarchical preconditions for virtue, and his defense of historical continuities seemed all the more impressive because he was looking at the traditional side of his own society. It was also significantly a society that remained open to piecemeal reform.

At the same time, I found in the Yale Sterling Library the original German edition, published soon after Hitler's accession to power, of Eric Voegelin's *Political Religions* (1938). Few books have shaped my historical awareness more decisively than this text, and I have never stopped applying Voegelin's insights about the mythical paradigms that inform modern political life. Moreover, the influence of Voegelin's work came after I had studied ancient Greek and after I had encountered the craft and fatalism of Thucydides. Thus, I applied both an ancient and a modern template to the examination of historical patterns and political motives. I suspect my longtime preoccupation with the snares of power, a trap that Thucydides identified with Atē, the goddess of mischief, came from reading the *Histories* as much as it did from listening to Marcuse. Indeed, it is hard for me to point to any single figure I studied or heard as a graduate student who exerted an overshadowing influence on my life to the exclusion of all other thinkers. Marcuse provided a vital impulse, a certain kind of intellectual stimulation, and a pedagogical model that were useful at a particular time. He was a doorway to other, more profound learning, but his role was limited for reasons that can be found in a passage I have asked my students to translate from Plato's *Criton*. "*Epeidē hē nosos enepipte kai diephtheire tēn polin, poi ēeistha su, poteron pros tous philous ē pros ton iatron* [If a plague befell and devastated the city to whom would you turn, your friends or the doctor]?" Criton's answer is "*pros ton iatron ēa—ēsan de entautha kai philoi. Ēdei gar ho iatros ta peri tēs nosou, empeiroteros on ē hoi alloi* [naturally I would go to the doctor, where I would find my friends. For the doctor would know about illness, being more knowledgeable than the others]."

Marcuse offered *philia* rather than *iatrikon*, which may be the reason that our relation could not evolve beyond a certain point. He was an older companion and one who caused me to look deeply into the history of European thought, but he could not treat the illness of the soul with the means at his disposal; nor could he explain the human condition more fully than what I had already learned from him at the age of twenty-three.

UNIVERSITY OF ROCHESTER

EUGENE D. GENOVESE
LATTIMORE 439

January 28, 1988

With deep regret I must confess to having read <u>Keeping the Tablets</u> with immense profit and, perhaps worse, with considerable pleasure--if I may except the customary madness on foreign policy. The Left will ignore this book only at its grave peril, for apart from the serious and often profound criticism it contains, it provides an invaluable guide to the nature of a formidable conservative coalition and to the relations of political forces therein.

Eugene D. Genovese,
Distinguished Professor of
Arts & Sciences in the
College of Arts & Sciences,
University of Rochester

IV

A Religious Visionary

Receiving a Will Herberg award as an outstanding teacher at the Intercollegiate Studies Institute's fiftieth-anniversary luncheon led me to recall the figure in whose name that award had been created. Will Herberg (1906–77) had been my own, informal teacher; and another recipient of the award, Peter Stanlis, could make the same claim with equal validity. Peter and I developed a friendship after I went to Rockford College in 1973, partly through our shared friendship with Will. When our mentor became sick shortly afterwards with what turned out to be a fatal brain tumor, both of us grieved, and until his death we made regular attempts to gather information about his condition. Peter and I also had wives who were fond of Will. He invariably treated these ladies in a gallant manner, one that strongly contrasted with his rumpled clothes and unkempt beard. By then a widower who had dedicated his life to the mountains of books in his apartment in Madison, New Jersey, Will enjoyed the company of women, on whom he would dote for hours. He would joke that these beauteous creatures had wasted their lives on irksome young intellectuals when they could have chosen him, a truly mature partner.

Will and I came to know each other in 1971, after I had called him as one of his appreciative readers and after I had moved to within about twenty miles of his home in New Jersey, where he taught at Drew University. For several years, we spoke on the phone regularly, exchanged notes, and had lunch or dinner together, typically at my house, a situation that I facilitated by picking Will up and after dinner driving him back home. His knowledge of technology was shockingly medieval, and each time he rode in our Volvo he discovered something new about modern automobiles, which is to say about those which had been manufactured since the '40s. My wife Dana joked that although Will as a Marxist had supposedly believed in "scientific socialism," he had obviously not taken seriously the Industrial Revolution and its effects.

At that time I was harder to take as a dinner companion than I have become in my nonage. Having already lost one junior professorship at Case Western Reserve and being on the verge of losing a second one at NYU, in both cases for blatantly ideological reasons, I was full of righteous anger against the evil academics who were then corrupting American youth. I was also disappointed that President Nixon, for whom I had voted in 1968, was not cleaning out those in higher education who were causing the corruption. (I had foolishly hoped that Nixon would turn out to be the authoritarian right-winger and stand-in for Joe McCarthy that my colleagues had feared he was.)

Will listened patiently to my rant before breaking in to observe that I possessed a paradigmatic "jecke" (German-Jewish) personality. Teutonic pedantry and Jewish moral righteousness seemed equally distributed in my approach to political and cultural issues. Since what he said was indisputably true, I could not argue back and therefore allowed him to speak uninterrupted. Will reminded me that whether one were a Marxist, as he had been in a previous incarnation, or a believer in divine providence, as he was now, one would have to come to terms with "History." Universities were not bad simply because obnoxious people taught there but because they had ceased to transmit "the funded wisdom of the past" and were trying to discredit and dismantle that wisdom. That would change, however, if the public made this a critical political issue. Otherwise the academic culture would likely remain the same, whether or not we had jobs. I have now adopted this view. Like Will, I am ready to battle for what is right in my vocation but have given up the naïve belief that appointing a few decent teachers here or there can alter the general academic climate. Only a political and cultural sea change can bring that about.

On one very big matter I have come to differ from my teacher. In *The Search for Historical Meaning*, I explored the observation that Will viewed American society more optimistically than I did. In his book *Protestant, Catholic, Jew* (1955), he saw distinctive American religious communities as leading toward assimilation into a shared American culture and polity. Behind these plural paths toward Americanization was a Judeo-Christian ethic and identity, which instilled unity at the price of a certain theological thinness. What Herberg emphasized in his religious sociology was the drive toward a common American identity, which all of the major religions were supposedly encouraging. As one listened to Jewish civic and religious leaders bewail Mel Gibson's film on the Passion, taken mostly from the Gospel of Matthew, and as one encounters the rejection of "Judeo-Christian" social ethics in mainline Protestant denominations, one wonders how much of this prediction has come true. In my view, Will focused too much on the cultural unity that came from a now dwindling middle-class consensus in the U.S. because he wished to believe that a unity based on his principles would prevail in America. The cultural disintegration, often resembling an autoimmune disease, and the victimological hysteria that I have portrayed in my books would have clashed with his vision of America as a synthesis of traditional cultures.

My point is not to treat this teacher as a Pollyanna (his optimism did diminish after the rise of the counterculture), but to indicate exactly where our perspectives diverged. Although we were both historically centered traditionalists who admired the bourgeois civilization that had dominated the West in the nineteenth century, Will had a stronger confidence than I that the good things would endure. The reason was partly personal, based in his own wrestling with Communist ideology and his movement toward a highly syncretistic religious outlook, one that incorporated Christian and Hebraic truths without recognizing the tensions between them. Although I wished the world were the way he viewed it, I am more drawn in my understanding of social history to friend/enemy antagonisms than I am to the peaceful interpenetration of great traditions.

Significantly, Will embraced his optimistic historical perspective because of a belief in providence. He believed that in some sense God would look after a country that had been good to him and his family, which had fled the chaos of post–World War I Europe to come to the U.S. And, unlike me, he thought that our countrymen, whom he identified with heartland Middle Americans, would ultimately reject the pernicious subversion of their social institutions. If only he had been right! The social class on which he and I both once pinned our hope of national regeneration, those whom we jokingly referred to as "the Archie Bunkers," has gone the way of the dinosaur. It has been replaced by a multitude of vastly more radicalized versions of Meathead, Archie's fashionably liberal son-in-law who by now could be an editorial writer for the *Wall Street Journal*.

Another reason the question of Will's relevance has stayed with me is an exchange that I had with the sociologist Irving Louis Horowitz while preparing for his magazine *Society* a review of a biography of Will by a Connecticut historian, Harry Ausmus. Irving was puzzled that I felt such an attachment to my subject, whose work in religious sociology he thought had become dated. "Who cares about Herberg any more?" was Irving's crushing assessment of my onetime gray eminence. By saying this, he was not insulting Will's character but alerting me to the fact that his scholarship had ceased to be taken seriously in the sociology of religion. In my view, however, this opinion is a bit too sweeping and overlooks part of the reason that Will's works have not worn well (if that is indeed the case). He was a man of his times, which was postwar America, an era that has come to stand for what the U.S. since the '60s has sought to leave behind.

At the same time, trying to fit Herberg neatly into the present American age as some kind of democratic pluralist is equally misleading. Murray Friedman, in an extended defense of his subjects in *The Neoconservative Revolution* (2005), refers to Will as "a premature neoconservative" and as a trailblazer for the rise of the neoconservative movement in the 1970s. The trouble with this attribution is that it is based on sociological overlap rather than on any precisely defined intellectual affinities. Because of Herberg's ethnicity, youthful involvement with the revolutionary Left, and acquaintance with later neoconservatives, particularly Sidney Hook, Friedman associates him with the eventual neoconservative ascendancy over the American Right. But unlike the neoconservatives, with the possible exception of Irving Kristol, Herberg was not fiercely opposed to Joe McCarthy, whom he regarded in his published statements as a mere "buccaneer," a silly politician whom the liberal establishment was raging against for its own purposes. Unlike the neoconservative Ronald Radosh, moreover, Will did not believe that McCarthy stood for an aberrant anticommunism, one that did the country considerable harm by deviating rightward from the policies of the Truman administration. From what I can recall, Will regarded McCarthy with a certain degree of amusement, and although he was never what has been called an "apocalyptic anticommunist," he often stated that anti-McCarthyites were at least as soft on Communist subversion as the Wisconsin senator had claimed.

I never heard Will complain about anti-Semitism or stress the need for American Jews to rally around the Israeli government. What for neoconservatives would be even more inconceivable, he had nice things to say about the anti-Zionist American Council for Judaism, a once thriving organization of American Reform Jews, mostly of German descent, who lived (or used to live) disproportionately in the American South. In Will's view, these council members were well-meaning American Jewish patriots who failed to recognize the power of Jewish nationalism after the Holocaust. Never did he describe this group or any other group of Jews as "self-hating." While neoconservatives Charles Krauthammer, George Will, and David Horowitz viewed the civil-rights movement (perhaps in some cases after the fact) as a defining moral experience, Will never saw that movement as a generally positive development.

Although Will voted for John F. Kennedy in 1960 and cheered on what he archaically styled "the labor movement," he viewed the Negro's demand for political rights with indifference—and even outright annoyance. He cited in support of his views comments that had been made in 1963 by Norman Podhoretz about Negro violence in New York. Will was particularly proud of an essay he had published in *National Review* (July 1964) titled "A Religious 'Right' to Violate the Law?" about the heretical Christianity preached by Martin Luther King Jr. He never wavered in his negative view of this civil-rights icon, who by the '80s had achieved posthumous sanctity in neoconservative circles.

Although it is possible to find like-minded views on the same subjects among other conservatives in the 1970s and even later, what has befallen Will is different from the fate of, say, someone like William F. Buckley Jr. Will has been claimed for a later phase of the postwar conservative movement to which he did not belong, and whose vague beginnings he had only begun to glimpse. As an intellectual historian and his younger friend, I think this act of preemption has interfered with a proper appreciation of his thinking. Having surveyed recent changing interpretations of his positions, I remain impressed by George Nash's interpretation of Will in *The Conservative Intellectual Movement in America* (1976). Nash, a true practitioner of the historian's craft, allows his subjects to speak for themselves and never tries to wedge them clumsily into an updated doctrinal framework.

Another vivid memory of Will concerns his penchant for collecting books, which filled every nook of his apartment and which my wife and I feared would create an avalanche if there were any sudden vibrations. He regarded his books as something special, and if at all possible he would try to limit his research to those bulky volumes lining his wobbly shelves. While after his death most of them landed in the Drew University Library, across from his rented rooms, Will avoided visiting that building if he thought a particular book he was looking for was somewhere in his collection. At one time in the hoary past, "my books," as he referred to them, had been shelved according to topics, but by the time I was granted the privilege of looking at them in the early '70s, their sheer mass had overwhelmed the semblance of order that Will had tried to establish.

Will had spent most of his adult life outside of academic institutions. He therefore valued his own research materials. His painstaking examinations of religion and religious sociology and his persistent study of languages, both ancient and modern, depended almost entirely on what he had acquired, often in secondhand bookstores and later as religion editor for *National Review*. Despite his erudition, a quality demonstrated in his learned efforts to reconcile Einstein's theory of relativity with Marxian materialism while a student leader of the Young Communists, Will never considered universities and university libraries to be specifically suited for his intellectual needs. And though a spirited and engaged teacher who was beloved by his graduate students, he spoke about his teaching as being only one of the several vocations he had practiced since leaving the Communist Party.

Another quality of Will's, and one that sometimes took amusing forms, was his loyalty to students and benefactors. He stood behind those he had personally educated and took great pains to help them with their careers. Above all, he was generous with his advice, whether or not the recipient had any desire to hear it. Will once took under his wing a young radical undergraduate at Drew, who was impressed by the fact that Will, as a young Communist, had called for the overthrow of the capitalist system. Instead of telling the disheveled youth that he had renounced the Communist Party and all of its works decades before, Will urged him to become a "true Communist of the old school" by bathing and grooming himself and studying hard for his classes. As a young Marxist, Will explained, he had applied himself to mathematics and logic in order to make himself into a better "scientific" socialist. If he had dared to look and smell like his young advisee, he would have been bounced out of the movement, which prided itself on its puritanical appearance. The student took seriously at least part of this advice and began attending classes again—and doing his homework. Indeed, he thereafter became so engrossed in mathematical theory that he no longer had the time to participate in protest demonstrations. What I could never determine, however, is whether Will got this student to bathe.

During Will's transition from his Communist past to what he later became, he had obtained a job, somewhere on the fringes of legality, working as a bookkeeper for a Mafia capo in northern New Jersey. Despite their differing backgrounds, Will and his employer became fast friends, and Will would habitually refer to his benefactor as a "solid family type" who had taught him, while he was his bookkeeper, "certain lessons about life." When that capo died (apparently of natural causes), Will was understandably grieved. Whenever we passed the restaurant near his apartment where they had dined, he reminisced about the time they had spent there. "The last time we ate in this place," he once pointed out, "it was really a sad thing. They were about to execute someone who was with us, and the poor fellow knew exactly what was going to happen."

"Why would they kill this fellow?" I asked rather indignantly. "He probably had a family and possibly small kids?"

Will looked at me in a puzzled way and then responded: "I'm sure they had their reasons. My boss didn't make those decisions lightly." Although he was the last person I could imagine rubbing someone out, Will was expressing loyalty to the person who had taken a chance on him and had furnished him with a job for which he had no technical training. But even more noticeable in this awkward attempt to defend the morally questionable was Will's lack of pretense. He never dropped names in order to make himself seem more important. And he never repudiated friendships that had ceased to be professionally useful. In this attribute Will stood out as a shining exception to many others I have come across throughout my professional career. The moral distance between him and the aspiring young academics whom I had met before encountering Will was obvious and unsettling. While these acquaintances had combined social climbing with radical posturing, Will was a thoroughly unpretentious social reactionary.

Another attribute that his friends and students often noted about Will was the otherworldly simplicity that marked his daily life. His friend Bob Schadler, who was then associated with ISI, once remarked jokingly that Will did "not even know how to be a consumer. Buying stuff [except for used books] was quite foreign to his nature." The rabbinical text *Ethics of the Fathers* answers the question "Who is a wise man?" with the appropriate response: "He who is happy with his portion." In Will's case, it is impossible to believe that he was not happy with what he had. Indeed, it is inconceivable that he ever coveted the material possessions of anyone else—or would have known how to take advantage of them had they fallen into his hands.

Once while he was eating in our home, my daughter, who was then a toddler, spilled a bottle of soda pop over Will's tuna casserole. (Will was then engaged in a conversation that absorbed his total attention.) He continued to eat without perceiving what had been done to his food, although he did comment later about how well-seasoned the main course was.

Although his essays, and particularly those on the uses of religion in the civil-rights movement, were among the best to appear in *National Review*, even when that publication was at its intellectual zenith, it is doubtful that Will received much in the way of compensation—or that he was even bothered by the meagerness of his recompense.

He expressed his views with a sense of conviction that others never forgot. Once, when asked how she thought Saint Paul might have looked, Ursula Niebuhr famously responded, "exactly like Will Herberg." Reinhold Niebuhr's wife proceeded to explain that Paul had been an impassioned Jew, full of moral energy, who focused on his conversion from error, and Will personified this religious type with a certain scriptural authenticity. My colleague Wes McDonald and I often recall the fury into which Will could be driven by even a casual reference to the disciples of Ayn Rand or her gospel of egotism. Wes remembers one ISI seminar at which Herberg attacked a Randian student who was dressed in black and glorifying self-interest. When Will argued that the government should support unemployed mine workers until they could acquire the skills to find new employment, the Randian in attendance jumped to his feet and proclaimed that the workers should be allowed to starve. Whereupon Will exclaimed in contempt: "That's barbaric, barbaric!" Despite his usual kindly manner, Will had zero patience for radical individualists, especially for the ones who strutted around mouthing platitudes.

He also liked to converse while eating, a habit that gave rise to all kinds of interesting anecdotes. His eating style, Wes recalls, led sometimes to socially bizarre situations. Will was once eating spaghetti marinara while engaged in conversation with his young charges. By the end of his impromptu lecture, he was covered with the sauce that had once been on his plate. Dining in the sense that George Santayana had in mind when he called it "an aesthetic act" was utterly foreign to Will's being.

I have speculated from time to time on whether Will might have been different if his life had taken another path: e.g., if his wife, who died when he was middle-aged, had lived longer; or if he had not been a serious young Communist but, like most professors of my acquaintance, an academic climber who merely toyed with being radical. What would his fate have been if he had not expressed politically incorrect opinions after he had turned rightward? As someone who has come to resemble him in more ways than I would have thought possible thirty years ago, I would have to answer: We are what we are. Had I chosen to be a Communist, I might have followed in the footsteps of Will in his radical youth. I would not have denied, any more than he did, the democratic centralism characteristic of the "Soviet experiment." I too might have rushed, with the same grim determination he once exhibited, to defend Lenin's suppression of the Kronstadt uprising, that abortive rebellion which sailors mounted against the Soviet regime in 1921. I too might have remarked that eggs had to be shattered for the sake of a revolutionary omelet. Will always complained, and with good reason, long after he had ceased to be a Communist, that would-be Marxist revolutionaries pretended that their plan did not involve violence—that they were simply in favor of putting into practice the Sermon on the Mount. Will never suffered from this childish illusion, no matter how deeply misguided his worldview once was.

Because he had drunk the cup of revolutionary socialism to the dregs, Will recovered from his ideological frenzy without a hangover. Like Dostoyevsky's atheist, who "stands at the penultimate stage to the most perfect faith," Will saw beyond the condition to which he had succumbed. He was not a half-recovered leftist. The same description applies to James Burnham, another former Communist (albeit in his case a recovered Trotskyite) and someone whom I met in the 1980s. One reason that both of these acquaintances of mine had recovered from their youthful obsessions, I have always suspected, is that, contrary to the impressions they tried to convey, neither had been a real leftist. Although neither dissembled when he joined a revolutionary movement, these men never belonged to the Left in any truly emotional sense. Their views as revolutionary socialists came from a false conception of History as Science, but that youthful mistake should not be confused with being a leftist of the heart. It is hard to imagine that either Will or Burnham was once intoxicated with the dream of a universal regime dedicated to egalitarian values. It is equally hard to believe that either man ever thought that the fulfillment of his historical schemes would help produce altruistic human beings.

Will's hard-nosed historical outlook, combined with his moral intensity and indifference to material comfort, was clearly a defining characteristic of his life. It went back into his Marxist period, and it continued to show up in his later years, after he had settled down to his lectures and writing. Will's evolution was an extension and refinement of what he had been all along. He was essentially the same person whose image was captured in a picture taken while he had been a Young Communist activist, a photo that I discovered while paging through John Patrick Diggins's study *Up From Communism* (1975). All that differed about his appearance by the time I got to know Will was the whiteness of his beard. It had been a very dark brown during his period of revolutionary militancy. The rest of his visage seemed to have remained unchanged, like his unchanging steely integrity and his perpetually exuberant personality.

WILL HERBERG
17 MADISON AVENUE 52
MADISON, N. J. 07940

DREW UNIVERSITY
MADISON, N. J. 07940

20 August 1971

Prof. Paul Gottfried
145 North Euclid Avenue
Westfield, N.J. 07090

Dear Professor Gottfried

I received your letter with the enclosed material this morning, for which much thanks. I have already begun reading your articles with great interest; I had already seen the piece in Modern Age when the issue appeared last year, but I did not know who the author was. Incidentally, the next issue of Modern Age will contain an article by me, "The 'What' and the 'How' in Ethics"; I'd be interested in your opinion.

On Sunday, the day after tomorrow, I'll be leaving to lecture at two ISI summer institutes (you know what these are?), one in the midwest and the other on Long Island, where I'll be lecturing on political philosophy. I'll be away two weeks. But I had already, after our phone conversation, gotten in touch with my connections on various nearby campuses, including Drew, and told them about you. As soon as I get back, I will take steps to pursue the matter. What you said on the phone, your curriculum vitae, and the articles you've sent me, confirm my desire to do what I can to help you get a good and permanent position in this area. You'll hear from me again some time after September 10th. And I am looking forward to meeting you very soon.

Yours faithfully,
Will Herberg

I am having your vita xeroxed.

Could you send me an offprint of your "Notes on Academic Unrest", Canadian Political Forum June 1969

V

A Flamboyant Friend

As I reflect on my friendship with Paul Piccone (1940–2004), I think of a flag that he gave me, or more exactly a flag that I got him to surrender to my care and that hangs on a wall adjacent to my study. It is the red, white, and blue flag of the Lega Nord, the northern Italian secessionist movement founded in Milan, which Piccone, although a central Italian, supported as an outspoken decentralist. When I requested the flag, which had been hanging in the office of his *Telos* magazine, Paul was recovering from an operation to remove a cancerous tumor from his forehead. He seemed in good spirits; he and his wife Mary were convinced that the surgery and radiation had dealt effectively with the freak growth that had "simply popped up." Alas, it returned, and within sixteen months of my last visit, Paul's remarkable life had ended at age sixty-four.

I would not have taken that flag of the Lega if I had known it was the only one in Paul's possession. It is anything but an attractive ensign, consisting of washed-out colors with a red cross in the background and a faded blue knight in the middle of the field. I had joked with Paul about the flag's appearance when it first caught my eye, noting that for Italians, an artistic people, "*Ciò infatti una bandiera brutta*" (That's a really bad flag). Paul, who like my father was extraordinarily generous, took the flag off the wall, folded it, and placed it into my hands. Together with a prayer card I received at his funeral, it is something that I continue to associate with my friend's departure from this world and with the bands of followers who used to come to visit him.

Paul was so much what he seemed to be that it is hard to imagine that such human beings exist. He came from the hills of Abruzzi, the mountainous region located east of Rome, and despite his family's decision to come to the U.S. when he was 15, he retained close connections with his boyhood home in L'Aquila even after the deaths of his parents. He spent part of every year in Italy, spoke English with an unmistakable Abbruzzese accent, and when he finally married at the advanced age of fifty-seven, he bemoaned the fact that his spouse Mary and her parents and brothers communicated in an alien south Italian dialect. His Latin ebullience, which was apparent to anyone who had ever stumbled upon him, took distinctive forms. Amidst a debate about political theory, he might burst into a stream of disconnected phrases punctuated by startling obscenities and by equally startling references to German metaphysical terms, all pronounced with his inimitable Italian regional accent. No one, however, seemed to be offended or astonished by these outbursts, which would simply subside, and at which point the conversation or editorial-board meeting would resume.

Another expression of Paul's exuberance was the generosity he would lavish on guests, even the ones who invited themselves. He would take them out to dinner, or else he and Mary would prepare feasts for their guests in their apartment on East 12th Street in Manhattan. Presumably the guests would stay in one of the several bedrooms in the Piccone apartment, which was situated next to a dwelling of Salesian nuns, until they decided to go home. If that meant somewhere in Europe, then Paul would pick up his guests at JFK and after their visit dutifully drive them back for the return flight. The many-coursed meals (*pranzi di molte portate*) that Paul and his wife served in their apartment intrigued me because of the variety of appetizing foods and fruity wines. There were so many delicacies before and after the pasta that the main course seemed almost irrelevant. Paul not only ate vigorously but also covered most of his food with mountains of salt. Such a practice horrified me, given the fact that Paul was chubby and would sweat profusely when he moved about quickly or lapsed into invectives against liberal modernity. Ironically, this lifestyle did nothing to impair his health and if it were not for the "freak tumor" on his forehead, he would still probably be gorging himself on pasta smothered in salt. How I wish this were the case!

During some of our get-togethers I had the sense that I had fallen into Paul's social and professional world after it had already taken definitive form. I once pointed this out to him when he and some of his friends, from Washington University in St. Louis, where he had taught, began talking about their friendship with sociologist Alvin Gouldner. They then went on to reminisce about how they had formed their journal, *Telos*, in Buffalo in 1968. I jokingly used a term drawn from Heidegger's *Being and Time* (1927), "*Geworfenheit*"—that is, being thrust into one's mode of existence at the time of birth—to refer to my being present in this unusual but already well-delimited society. The social circle around Paul had been obviously thriving for years before my arrival on the scene. My wife Mary always referred to "that New York crowd" whenever I said I was going into the city for an editorial meeting.

Not everyone in the group still lived in New York, and such editors as Frank Adler, Russell Berman, David Pan, Joe Bendersky,

Victor Zavlasky, David Ost, Gabor Rittersporn, and Tim Luke, all of whom I met at Paul's apartment, had either moved from the Big Apple or had never resided anywhere within a few hundred miles of it. But there was always a place for me to stay when I came. Gary Ulmen and the widow of my friend Jim Novak (Michael's brother), Naomi, were New Yorkers; and Mary and I would stay with one of these friends when we sojourned in Manhattan. Although Gary was closely connected to *Telos* and was probably Paul's closest friend, Naomi, like Mary, had only a distant and precarious relation to the "New York crowd." Both of these ladies viewed this circle of friendship with a certain wonder mixed with annoyance.

It never became quite clear how Paul's magazine kept financially solvent—or whether it even sold the five thousand or so copies that came out quarterly. There were also elaborate newsletters that members of the inner circle supervised. I had no idea who made up the shortfalls that *Telos* publications, which included books, must have incurred. Paul acquired a house and further office space, furnished with state-of-the-art equipment for his publications, in Candor, New York, about twenty miles south of Ithaca, but I doubt that any of these investments paid for themselves. Moreover, as the magazine began to swerve away from the academic Left, it lost many of its original readers. *Telos* originally defined itself explicitly as anti-Soviet, yet theoretically pro-Marxist and pro–Frankfurt School. But as the publication, under Paul's direction, moved toward a decentralist, communitarian position, it eventually ceased to be identified with the Left. My association with the magazine from the late 1980s on undoubtedly weakened even further its reputation as a progressive journal.

My fellow editors never struck me as academic climbers. Although some of them—Berman, his former student David Pan, Frank

Adler—had managed to create for themselves distinguished professorial careers, they hardly ever mentioned their career concerns in conversation with me. Neither Paul nor Gary Ulmen held a university post, and most of the other editors seemed like people who taught somewhere or had once done so, *faute de mieux*. They also enjoyed debating ideas in a way that few of my academic associates did. I still recall a winter meeting that Paul had called in his newly constructed "bunker" in Candor, which as he told us was "situated midway between his apartment in New York and his in-laws' place in Toronto." By the time we got there, the temperature had plummeted to twenty degrees below zero, and a snowstorm was predicted for the next day. We stayed in Candor arguing about some counterfactual—for example, whether it would have been better if the printing press had never been invented, and whether that question would be appropriate for some future issue of *Telos*—until the snow began to fall heavily. Although Mary called to warn that I had better leave at once because of the accumulation of snow south of the New York–Pennsylvania line, I decided to sit through the discussion and leave the next morning. Everyone who remained had to drive hundreds of miles through a blizzard that Sunday but no one seemed to care. When I spoke to Paul a few days later, all he remembered was that I was "a damned liberal idiot" for sticking up for literacy during our Saturday evening dinner.

Although his funeral took place on a sultry July afternoon, I continue to associate Paul with wintry weather. The return trip from Candor involved driving at my own peril along roads that had been closed by the police; moreover, I had lost my car key in the icy snow upon arriving in Candor and then spent several hours getting a duplicate made at a Mazda distributor in Ithaca. In 1991, we had held a *Telos* conference in Elizabethtown, before my family and I had moved to central Pennsylvania, in winter weather that was equally challenging. During that conference it was so cold that walking from the campus to the hotel on the main street, where our attendees were lodged, was like a medieval form of torture. On the second and last night, the heating at Wohlgemuth's (a Pennsylvania Dutch inn that at the time had antiquated wiring) went off suddenly, and some of the guests chose to sleep in their cars rather than risk staying in their rooms and presumably freezing to death. Gary Ulmen told me the next morning that he had spent most of the night trying to fall asleep under a pile of clothes that he had brought along. When he finally succeeded, he was awakened by the cries of someone, perhaps the town drunk, stumbling along in the icy night and crying for some absent female named "Sarah." Gary's story about Sarah made such an impression on us that thereafter we came to refer to our wintry conference as "the Sarah experience."

Rummaging through my file case recently, I came across a diatribe by Danny Postel that appeared in *In These Times* (April 24–30, 1991). A self-described Marxist, Postel went after Paul for having presumed to publish my writing, and in particular my qualified defense of Heidegger against Heidegger's Marxist critic Victor Farias. Although Postel expressed the curious belief that I shilled for the Heritage Foundation (an institution that would have found my views even more obnoxious than he did), he did a good job summarizing those pieces in *Telos* which he found offensive. I had indeed "claimed to detest the bureaucratic welfare state for its uprooting of the family and traditional community" and I had suggested (or at least I might have) that I was "more afraid of the meddling bureaucrats in the Equal Opportunities Commission than of recrudescent Klan violence." I had also indicated that the present fuss over Heidegger was caused not by his lapse of decency in joining the Nazi Party but by his obvious contempt for what had become politically fashionable in recent years.

I was not saying that those values Heidegger had opposed were necessarily bad. But I was trying to understand the united front that had suddenly formed against his thought, and which was playing up what had long been known about his opportunistic kowtowing to the Third Reich. That front extended from Straussians and neoconservatives to Marxists and quasi-Marxists. I also alluded in my commentary to Heidegger's lectures on Nietzsche, given in 1936–37, which were first published in 1951 and represented an implicit attack on the Third Reich. How else could one understand Heidegger's extended tirade against the "will to power" in Nietzsche as a false path toward *das Sein*, except as an assault on the obvious exercise of tyrannical power by Hitler?

Piccone, who was the other object of Postel's attack, made clear that he had no deep interest in Heidegger, but he had encouraged me to defend him against questionable accusations. An admirer of the great phenomenologist Edmund Husserl, Piccone believed that Heidegger had distorted the thought of his onetime mentor—not to mention the fact that he had stripped Husserl, who was a Protestant of Jewish parentage, of certain university privileges after Heidegger became rector at Freiburg in 1933. But Paul was a true defender of both intellectual freedom and the right of a falsely accused thinker to be defended by someone who was willing and able to do so. What makes Postel's polemic particularly memorable, and the reason I am giving it so much space, is not only that it cemented my friendship with Paul, but also that it represented the replacement of one Left by another. Those for whom Postel spoke were the antifascist cultural Marxists, the despisers of bourgeois Christian civilization who were only secondarily Marxists. Paul, even in his radical phase, was interested in class structure and the apparent contradictions of capitalism. It is impossible to imagine that he ever cared about the supposed remnants of "fascist attitudes" in middle-class society or about the anti-Semitism supposedly built into anticommunism.

According to Postel, Piccone had deviated from the Left even more glaringly in other ways. Taking his cue from "Gary Ulmen, the main catalyst behind *Telos*'s rehabilitation of Schmitt," Paul was glorifying the "Nazi intellectual" who "authored no fewer than five books and 35 tracts in support of Hitler's regime during the period of 1933–36." Although it is doubtful that Schmitt produced in this period as many tracts as Postel contends or that what he published was as consistently pro-Nazi as we are told, what is correct is that *Telos* from the late '80s onward spearheaded the introduction of Schmitt's ideas into American intellectual circles. And Piccone and Ulmen did so while ignoring the admonitions of Richard Wolin and other PC leftists cited by Postel who purported to have located Nazi tendencies in Schmitt's thought from the 1920s on.

Postel goes on to comment on the "long, strange trip" that had taken the editors of *Telos* from Marxist beginnings toward their present questionable company. He praises Piccone's early contribution to leftist thought, "Phenomenological Marxism," an essay that had graced an anthology, *Toward a New Marxism*, that *Telos* had produced in 1970. And he quotes Piccone's remark as late as 1987 about how his journal had been launched with "a systematic effort to retrieve the lost and suppressed tradition of Western Marxism." This endeavor had guided its issues into the 1980s. Such efforts showed that *Telos* remained committed to "socialism—indeed to some reconstructed version of Marxist theory," even if the magazine's founder had emphatically rejected the orthodox Marxism taught in the Soviet bloc. And unlike European Marxists, Postel might have added, Piccone spared no venom when he called attention to the evils of communism in practice.

By 1987, however, according to Postel, Piccone had given ample signs of ceasing to be a Marxist. In a newsletter that year he criticized his editorial board for lacking focus and he closed his message with this provocative thought: "What I think has happened is that, with the disappearance of any meaningful political 'movement' and the abandonment of the Marxist paradigm, we have scattered in many directions—not always necessarily compatible." Piccone proceeded to pose a question that would reemerge in later conversations with his fellow editors: "What do we stand for and what are we attempting to accomplish with *Telos*?" The same turning-point question came up again in the Fall 1994 issue, which carries the title "Is There a Telos left in *Telos*?" Playing on the Greek word for purpose or end, Piccone's editorial note makes clear that if the magazine is to remain relevant, it should address a critical post-Marxist issue, namely, how can "federal populism," or a decentralized approach to local self-government, be made to work. By 1994, the abandonment of the search for "a lost Marxist tradition" had given way to a very different telos: the unmasking of bureaucratic structures that stood in the way of renewed, self-governing communities.

I witnessed the effects of this turning when I first met Paul face-to-face in 1987. Our very first conversation, over the phone, took place when I was working as a senior editor at *The World and I* in Washington, D.C. I had just read an essay of Paul's (I soon began calling him Paolo to distinguish him from myself) that one of my assistants had solicited. With his customary rapid diction punctuated by Italian pronunciations, Paul characterized himself as a "Marxist who is really on the left." This amazed me, I explained, since I considered myself a member of the American Old Right but apparently held the same views as he did. "How is it," I asked, "that you and I can agree on so much while claiming to be on opposite sides politically?" Paul responded, "[b]ecause you're a Marxist but don't know it."

A few weeks later I stopped off in New York to meet him and his alter ego, Gary Ulmen. I had also agreed to join the two that evening at a *Telos* forum that would be widely attended by their local groupies. Again I was astonished that while I generally saw eye-to-eye with both of my interlocutors, I inclined toward Paul, who still called himself a Marxist, more than toward Gary, who made no pretense of being a radical leftist. Paul went on, all the while plying me with espresso that would have awakened the dead, about the wily tactics of the managerial state, exemplified by its New Class defenders. This regime appealed to equality but sought to control our thoughts. Gary seemed to be less inclined toward this dark view than his companions, and he tried to present the American government as a general force for good. But Paul steadily interrupted him to express his mounting skepticism about the merits of the present state of American democracy.

By 1989, although it might have been sooner, it was possible no longer to associate Piccone in any way with the Left. In *Telos* 81 (Fall 1989), he poured ridicule on the "liberal left academic establishment" in terms that one might have expected to find in the columns of my now deceased friend Sam Francis. Sam had actually become a fan of Piccone's after receiving a copy of this blistering polemic, which he read with enthusiasm. He then kept in touch with the *Telos* circle for several years and participated as a panelist at one of its conferences on populism. Sam, who himself was always inveighing against the managerial state, seconded Piccone's observation that "the defeat of fascism and the successful containment of Stalinism implied a different periodization in terms of which the mediational stage of bureaucratized technocratic domination may be far from over." This long aside in a *Telos* editorial lent support to Sam's conviction and later informed my own work that took form under the influence of Piccone, namely *After Liberalism*. Paul (who may have been my only reader to have stated anything so unconventional) considered my book to be "very soft criticism." No matter what I claimed to have achieved with this work, he told me, I had not launched an unequivocal assault on managerial domination.

Note that I am not pigeonholing Paul as a rightist who took years to recognize what he was. What I am arguing is something very different. Paul changed his political positions over the years and went from being a hero to Danny Postel to an object of inspiration for Sam Francis. But certain constant themes and reference points shaped his work—and caused his shifting. Piccone held a harsh view of bourgeois society and of those liberal constitutional forms in which it had organized itself. For Paul, there was no falling away from older liberal ideals that preceded the rise of modern managerial control. It was all part of the same process, and so Paul had no trouble finding kindred spirits among neomedieval Catholics or critical theorists. What informed his critical context was a negative view of where bourgeois modernity had been inevitably headed from the moment of its inception. In response to the German scholar Russell Berman, he published this prolix but revealing opinion in *Telos* 105 (Fall 1995): "Nationhood is a reification. Russell's critique of economic globalism is obviously on the mark but it applies as effectively to the nation. The kind of managerialization and cultural impoverishment globalism brings about through the market is precisely what nations are doing on a more limited scale. National and local particularity are two qualitatively different things." Furthermore: "Dialects, local customs, regional cuisine, particular traditions are either absorbed or deterritorialized in a national context" or reduced to "premodern anachronisms." Wherever the bourgeoisie was allowed to tread, one found an inescapable "flattening" and "homogenization."

Equally illustrating his standpoint were Piccone's comments about the Italian economic historian Luciano Pellicani, whom he knew well and who had looked for the origins of modern capitalism in late medieval Italy. Piccone applauded his fellow Italian for rejecting that most bourgeois of Teutonic celebrants of the old liberal order, Max Weber; nonetheless, he considered Pellicani to be overly sympathetic toward the economic process that he analyzed in his long study: "In recycling the libertarian illusion that the market as the universal organizational mechanism makes it possible for society to do away with all collective values, now privatized within the confines of particular individual projects, and in hypostatizing such a modernist remake of the old 'bourgeois' vision to the level of a universal culture, Pellicani has managed to outdo both Francis Fukuyama and Dr. Pangloss."

This constant antibourgeois perspective accounts for much in Piccone's critical commentaries that otherwise would be hard to grasp. He did not see much of a difference, for example (unless he was joking when he said this), between my historical and political views and those of our self-identified left-liberal editorial colleague David Ost. At the meeting in Candor in the late '90s, he kept insisting that Ost, an ardent feminist and outspoken human-rights exponent, and I were saying the same things in different words. We both seemed to believe that the postmedieval world was a social improvement over what it replaced and, even more damningly, that written constitutions had benefited particular societies. In "The Uses and Abuses of Schmitt" in *Telos* 122 (Winter 2002), which he coauthored with Ulmen, Piccone quoted *After Liberalism* and my writings on Schmitt—and even paid them modest tribute. But once having paid the devil his due, he let his readers know that he held no brief for my "bourgeois liberal" convictions. While Piccone and I often found ourselves agreeing about managerial tyranny and its successive forms of thought control, he could never quite get used to my nostalgia for a formerly functioning liberal world. It was one that had been marked by nation-states and the dominance of a bourgeois civilization.

Paul was also distressed that *Telos* contributors were presenting what looked like neo-Thomist natural law, a development that he complained about with increasing acrimony in the 1990s. His visceral dislike for universals sprang not from any nihilistic impulse but from the understandable suspicion that universalist moral thinking could lead to human-rights talk and from there into hardened ideological absolutes. In *Telos* 110 (Winter 1998), Paul, who was at most a very lax Catholic, prefaced an issue full of Catholic protests against modern and postmodern thinking with this admonition: "In a social context reduced to all-pervasive systems confronting hopelessly isolated and therefore abstract individuals, there is a strong temptation to appeal to transcendental norms whose internalized theological foundations make it appear as 'obvious.'" Although such appeals had served a good cause by "delegitimating Communist regimes," Paul warned against pushing them too far: "Human rights are either contractual, in which case they do not cut any ice with those who are not party to that contract, or 'transcendental,' in which case they can only apply to the particular cultures to which they are inextricably a part. To universalize them is nothing but an act of cultural imperialism."

Paul might have overreacted in this and in other statements to the application of moral absolutes, but the fear he expressed had some basis in fact. His opposition to the universalization or hypostatization of moral claims, a position that I challenged more than once in *Telos*, was based on his understanding of liberal imperialism, a tendency toward which he believed soi-disant traditionalist thinkers were being pulled. As soon as one accepted certain moral premises, went his argument, the grantor would be enlisted for a human-rights crusade under New Class guidance.

Although it is arguably possible to uphold cross-cultural moral norms without signing on to such an adventure, it was clear why Paul rushed to deny moral claims that were not contractually founded or situationally specific. In the face of a rising democratic messianism, he was making clear where he did not want to go. Even more important, he alluded to the problem that Carl Schmitt called the "tyranny of values," the tendency in a modern, individualistic society to privilege certain preferred values and to try to validate them by imposing them on others. Thus, women's rights or gay rights are elevated into something more than what a progressive majority would like to enforce in New York. They are turned into an eternal moral good, on behalf of which entire populations are to be mobilized, lest they show themselves to be morally deficient. This tendency for Piccone was something graver than a quirk of late modern culture. For him it lay at the heart of bourgeois civilization.

Looking at Paul's written expositions, which often feature clusters of technical-sounding phrases, I am struck by how much less interesting they seem than his torrential outbursts at conferences. In one session on the Roman vs. the Greek model of governance held at Elizabethtown, Paul went into a hymn to the Roman spirit of empire that might have been lifted from the thunderous orations of Benito Mussolini. He then contrasted the Roman sense of command and Rome's development of universal legality to the oddities of Greek civilization, "a culture that had been fashioned by sodomites who liked to write plays." Although a Hellenophile, I found this comment to be so outrageously funny that I couldn't stop laughing for an hour after I had heard it. At a later conference in Manhattan, Paul took me and Frank Adler (Gary and Russell Berman for some reason couldn't attend) to a kosher-style delicatessen somewhere in midtown for lunch. During that hectic meal Paul and Frank began to argue loudly about the possible contents of a special issue devoted to fascism and modernization, a theme that Frank, who had done a monograph on this subject, promised to work up into an entire issue.

As I listened to my luncheon companions screaming at each other about some esoteric historical topic while biting into their corned-beef sandwiches, I began to think about Woody Allen's movie *The Front*. In this film, which is executed with considerable humor and depicts the trials of Communist screenwriters during the McCarthy era, Allen has several of his protagonists meet at a Jewish dairy restaurant. There they affirm both their commitment to world socialism and their determination to sell their scripts to Hollywood. As this solemn conversation unfolds, the waiter who is bringing their breakfast orders interrupts the speakers. A middle-aged writer who has just sung hosannas to the workers' revolution suddenly shows alarm when he notices that his order of "scrambled eggs loose and lox" has gone to someone else at his table. He starts screaming that the order is his, but at the same time he tries not to let go of his previous, more exalted topic: the workers' struggle and his own willingness to sacrifice himself on its behalf.

In a similar way, Paul and Frank seemed to be suspended in the midtown delicatessen between two poles of interest, ones that were so far apart as to cause me profound amusement. One minute they were talking about corned beef and pickles and about the French fries that had never arrived; the next they were arguing in very loud voices about a radical Italian fascist, Giovanni Bottai, and whether he was really a Leninist pretending to be an Italian ultranationalist or whether the opposite was true. I've no idea how the other diners reacted to this conversation, which could not have been missed by those sitting at adjacent tables. For all I knew, these diners might have found the social interaction as hilarious as I did. When I later described the exchange to my wife and Naomi Novak, Mary attributed it all to "being in New York." Whereupon Naomi pointed out that she had lived in New York for decades but that she still found Paul and his visitors to be "original," even by the high local standards for weirdness.

Paul's inveterate distrust of the bourgeoisie and his theoretical quest to restore authentic (pre- or postbourgeois) community also determined how he read certain authors. For me, this was the most difficult aspect of our long-term friendship, for the two of us identified those thinkers we discussed with different ideas and themes. For example, Paul avoided speaking about Theodor Adorno as the editor of or as a major contributor to *The Authoritarian Personality*. The plea that runs through this volume for accelerated social engineering was not what Paul wished to identify with critical theory. Rather, he praised Adorno for his stark warning against mechanistic modernity in *Die Dialektik der Aufklärung*, for his authorship of *Negative Dialektik*, and for his critical commentary on Husserl's phenomenology. Piccone would allow essays to be inserted into his journal dealing with Adorno's musicology; nonetheless, he had no real interest in defending twelve-tone dissonance, except to whatever extent aesthetic subjects could be related to timely political issues. Paul was happy to have contributors expatiate on commercialized culture by referring to the Frankfurt School's critique of the "*Kulturbetrieb*." Critical theory from his point of view was not something to be studied as a detached scholarly exercise. It was only useful if it illuminated existential questions and pointed the way out of historical problems.

This raises the question of whether one can reasonably locate Paul on any current political spectrum. During the time I knew him, he inclined somewhat toward the parties of the European populist right, but he also found fault with them and their leaders, whom he flooded with billingsgate at a distance of thirty-five hundred miles. He detested self-described "national" movements as vehicles of French revolutionary ideology; and therefore even when he expressed some preference for a populist cause, it was for parties like the Lega Nord rather than the Front National. While Paul despised the fascists, who wrecked his native land, he never mistook anti-immigrationists for Nazis. He believed that self-identifying communities had a right to decide who should or should not be allowed to join them. The rub for him was that national governments were both destroyers of communities and convenient rallying points against internationalist structures that he sometimes distrusted more than nation-states. But for a while, to my utter amazement, Piccone supported the multicultural and politically correct EU as an instrument for breaking down national bureaucracies and for restoring regional and local identities. In a way that might have made sense to an early-nineteenth-century French or Italian counterrevolutionary transported to a later age, Paul ascribed Western political problems in the twentieth century, including Nazism and communism, to bourgeois incompetence or corruptness. Among the bad turns he was always coming back to were the Enlightenment (but not the Reformation, which seemed a suitable response to Catholic bureaucracy), the nation-state, human rights, and the global market. Paul would lay at the doorstep of these and other bourgeois inventions whatever had turned out badly in modern history. Most astonishing for me, he would take this perspective as someone who chose to live in the heart of an urban maelstrom in Manhattan. He wondered why I as a bourgeois liberal had not made a similar choice, to which my customary response was "because I prefer nineteenth-century Vienna or Paris to this hypermodern mess."

It is hard for me to imagine where Piccone would fit into a modern American political taxonomy. He and the historian Christopher Lasch noted over a decade ago, at a conference at Elizabethtown College, that Right and Left had become inextricably confused, and that it was not worth the effort to try to disentangle them. This observation has seemed increasingly true as the establishment political poles have become united by a shared adoration for global democracy, human rights, and, with few exceptions, a global consumer culture. Piccone and Lasch both observed that the differences now separating Left and Right had become utterly trivial in comparison to what they had been before.

Although critical of this process, Paul did take sides on practical issues, in a way that would suggest a growing proclivity toward the Republican Party. He expressed admiration for Rudy Giuliani for making it possible to walk on safe streets in New York City. He also endorsed the military responses of Bush the Elder and Bush the Younger to Saddam Hussein's aggression (or at least the appearance of aggression in 2003); and during the American-led liberation of Kuwait in 1991, Paul angered his old Marxist friends (and surprised me) by calling for a swifter and more complete retribution against the Iraqi invaders than the one that was then taking place. But such reactions did not indicate the waning of his stated anxiety about the disintegration of community in the West; nor did they suggest that Paul mistook present-day America for the best of all possible worlds. Such a world would have worn for him a premodern face, and he saw it realized, however imperfectly, when he spoke about his noisy, heavily traveled but distinctive neighborhood in Southeastern

Manhattan—or else when he reminisced about his beloved birthplace in the rugged hills of south-central Italy.

14.V.1998

Dear friend,

thank you ever so much for your letter and all the other pièces justificatives. Was ich da vom Elizabethtown höre ist haarsträubend, erinnert aber an den treffenden Ausdruck, den der Heimwehrführer Steidle für die Nazis gebraucht hatte:"wildgewordene Spießer". So treffend, daß der gute Mann nach dem Anschluß in das KZ DAchau kam, wo er umgebracht wurde. Il n'y a que la vérité qui blesse hat schon der alte Napoleon gesagt. Doch derSpießer kommt sich heute nur modern vor, wenn er blasphemieren kann ! Und modern muß er à tout prix sein !

Nein, die Nazis sind echteste Linke. Dazu gehört auch ein prononcierter "Antisemitismus". Monarchen und Päpste hatten immer ihre Hofjuden, Hocharistokraten ihre Hausjuden, Richard Roudenhove-Kalergi und Adalbert Sternberg wearen sogar Philosemiten und der "Semigotha" denunzierte die jüdischen Alliancen. (Leider haben immer zu viele Israeliten auf das falsche, d.h. linke Pferd gesetzt - auf die Demokratie, Sozialismus und Kommunismus. In meiner Schabbes-Predigt im Tempel Emmanu-El - größte Synagoge der Welt - habe ich dies 1981 erwähnt. (A Jew believing in democracy needs psychiatric treatment.) Die Leute waren begeistert !   Interessant war der Artikel von Kurth über die protestantische Politik Amerikas, den Sie nmir auch schickten. Er sagt aber auch nur die HALBE Wahrheit. Ich schickte "First Things" KÜRZLICH einen Artikel über die Reformation und die Moderne, in dem ich meine alte Ansicht von den Wurzeln der Moderne in der Reformation formell widerrief.(1996 pries der Bundespräsident Roman Herzog Luther als Urheber der Moderne - the opposite is true. Die Moderne kommt von der "Aufklärung" und diese hat ihre Wurzeln in einem deklassiert/en Zweig der Renaissance.) Ich bin sehr neugierig, ob FIRST THINGS das publizieren wird. Mein Stolz besteht darin, daß ich fast ein Drittel der Werke Luthers gelesen habe - das wären in toto 107 Bände a 600 Seiten !!! Von Indidividualismus keine Spur ! Wir standen immer für die Santa Anarchia católica ! Rum, Romanism and Rebellion ! Die Protestanten für Law and Order. Wer einen festen Boden unter den Füßen hat, kann nach allen Seiten ausschlagen ! Das wußte schon Keyserling.

In die USA komme ich am 8.X. für die Philadelphia Society in Wilmington. Interessant ist der neue Historiker Verein. Hat sehr wenige Katholiken - kenne nur John Lukács, den ich seinerzeit nach Chestnut Hill gebracht hatte, auch Gertrud Himmelfarb.

Gerade sah ich wieder meinen Enkel Paul Gottfriedowitsch!

VI

Three Central Europeans

The long, productive lives of Erik Maria Ritter von Kuehnelt-Leddihn (1909–99), Thomas Molnar (1921–), and John Lukacs (1924–) intersected biographically, geographically, and at least to some extent politically. All three had personal connections to Budapest, where the Tyrolean nobleman Kuehnelt-Leddhin studied between the wars. Lukacs and Molnar have also resided in the Hungarian capital (indeed Lukacs has the honor of being born there), and since the fall of the Communist regime, each has returned to lecture at its storied university founded in 1697 after Eugene of Savoy had liberated the Hungarian capital from the Turks. (As a child, I learned from my father that America's second oldest university, Yale, which was near our house in Bridgeport, had been established only four years after the reestablishment of Hungary's most famous university.)

As a (nonleftist) exile from the Nazis, in 1943 Kuehnelt-Leddihn took a post as a history professor at Chestnut Hill College, a Catholic girls' school just barely within the city limits of Philadelphia. From this scenic setting, he returned home to Lans, Austria, in 1947, while others, as Lukacs has noted, were still crossing the Atlantic in search of careers in the opposite direction. Before his journey home, Kuehnelt-Leddihn took measures to ensure that his successor in the history department would be John Lukacs, a Hungarian exile who had arrived in the U.S. in 1946 and who was destined for publishing fame in his adopted language. Kuehnelt-Leddihn was drawn to Lukacs, who, like himself, was a Central European Catholic, a former student at the University of Budapest, and someone who had taken strong stands against both the Nazis and the Communists. This kindness is acknowledged in Lukacs's autobiography *Confessions of an Original Sinner* (1990). One particularly apt description sums up Kuehnelt-Leddihn's attitude toward issues that mattered to him: "His mind was unusually independent: he was an avowed conservative, a monarchist, and an eloquent opponent of the ideology of modern democracy at a time when this was not only unpopular in the United States but virtually unheard of." As a friend of both Lukacs and Kuehnelt-Leddihn, I learned that they met only infrequently after 1956, despite their many transatlantic crossings. From all accounts, however, they remained on close personal terms.

Not so with Lukacs and Molnar, whose views have often sharply diverged. (Both figure prominently in Patrick Allitt's informative 1993 study *Catholic Intellectuals and Conservative Politics in America*.) Lukacs has pulled no punches when observing that Molnar seems to detest American politics and society. And Molnar has been harsh about his (part-time) adopted home in such French tracts as *Le modèle défiguré* (1986), *Américanologie: triomphe d'un modèle planétaire* (1991), and in other spirited polemics in English, French, and Hungarian. Molnar has never held back in mocking the "boy scout" mentality of American leaders and their "Disney World conceptions" of the democratic future. He has ridiculed the Protestant sectarian passions that he finds lurking behind the American democratic faith, and he has quipped that American materialism has gone from being a vice to a worldview.

Molnar and the Catholic apostle of American democratic capitalism Michael Novak stand at opposite poles in how they see the present age and Western history in general. Molnar's defense of Catholic traditionalism, and his call for a return of the West to a new interpenetration of religious and political institutions—a theme explored in, among other books, *Twin Powers: Politics and the Sacred* (1988) and *Authority and Its Enemies* (1976)—reveals his unmistakably Thomistic cast of mind. A secular society or one that tries to disencumber itself from theological reference points is for Molnar an unnatural thing. In his work there is an exploration of the kind of alliance of throne and altar that was favored by nineteenth-century European counterrevolutionaries. In *The Counterrevolution* (1969) Molnar excavates this starkly reactionary tradition and argues for its critical relevance for a morally and socially disintegrated Western civilization.

Such thinking is nowadays no more in fashion in Europe than it is in the U.S. From all accounts, Europeans surpass Americans in their ferocious secularism and acceptance of multiculturalism, which often lead them into granting carte blanche to Muslim fundamentalists. It is Novak, the celebrant of our late modernity and of its defining characteristics—a capitalist welfare state and human-rights doctrine—who today enjoys acceptability in America as the Catholic traditionalist. In a universe of discourse in which the pertinent ideological choices are a defense of a glorified present and movement in the direction of the multicultural Left, the conservative role has fallen to Novak by default.

What is left to Molnar is the job of noting, from the sidelines, the derailments of a mechanized and standardized society. I have recently reread an essay of his published in 1999, "L'âme et la machine," which offers devastating strictures against the "civilization of the machine." Although the arguments are not entirely original and bring to mind Heidegger and the French Calvinist theologian Jacques Ellul, Molnar puts his own spin on the already sounded warning against the rule of technique. He is especially convincing in pointing out the faith in an unfinished technological project that marks American society and culture. Those who express this vision are not totally dehumanized but deeply "emotional beings" who are seeking a post-Christian religious faith. Molnar's discussion about "thinking machines" puts me in mind of an academic project that is now taking off, which is to provide learning as "information" via the Internet, thereby saving the consumer the cost of college tuition while making available a streamlined form of mass education. Worship of machines, consumerism, and the drive for equal opportunity combine here to furnish a new model of education in which the human factor in transmitting "learning" is minimized.

Molnar is not playing an unusual role for a real man of the right. As an author who has been asked, "Do you give out suicide razors with your books?" I entirely commiserate with his predicament as a less-than-well-received prophet. It boggled my mind to learn that in 1964 Molnar made an unexpected appearance in Arnold Foster and Benjamin Epstein's turgid testimony to liberal intolerance, *Danger on the Right* (New York: Doubleday, 1964, 216), where he is placed among anticommunist Goldwaterites. My reaction was that his Anti-Defamation League critics were several centuries off in dating his extremism.

An even more tasteless attack on Molnar took place in my presence at Rockford College when Allan Bloom came there as a speaker in 1981. According to Bloom, who was then excoriating the "enemies of liberal democracy," Molnar "thought that Nazism would have been all right except for its choice of leaders." This remark was not only baseless but, even more disconcertingly, failed to take into account a grim historical fact. While Bloom spent the war years helping his father tend the grounds of the Jewish Community Center in Rockford, Illinois, Molnar was languishing in Dachau. The Nazis placed him there while he was a student in Belgium, after he had let his feelings be known about the immorality of Hitler's empire.

Before I met Molnar in 1982, in the small cluttered apartment that he occupied with his wife on West End Avenue in Manhattan's West Side, I received an immaculately written note in French. It indicated how I should let my host know that I had arrived at his building, so that he could then let me in. This eminent scholar, as I soon learned, lived among distraught elderly Jewish widows who greatly feared violent intruders. When I asked why he stayed there, he explained he was still teaching French at Brooklyn College. In any case, he could not abide the idea of moving into his wife's sporadically occupied house in northern New Jersey. Unlike Lukacs, who travels from his farmhouse in Chester County, Pennsylvania, to the Big Apple only on business, and Kuehnelt-Leddihn, who lived happily in the Tyrol, Molnar has remained an incorrigible urbanite. New York, Paris, and Budapest are the three cities that bound the geography of his soul. Once while I was driving him from Elizabethtown, Pennsylvania, where he had participated in a seminar on building a global society, to his in-laws in Damascus, Maryland, Thomas remarked that he had seen very little of America's rural scenery. I responded in jest that the reason might be the absence of an eighteenth-century peasant society and the appropriate *grands seigneurs*. Joseph de Maistre, the impassioned enemy of the French Revolution whom Molnar has praised in his defense of counterrevolutionary thinking, would have noted this deficiency had he been present on our trip.

Molnar's published work consists in part of a vigorous defense of Thomistic realism and polemics directed against late-medieval nominalism and its supposed ramifications. My desk drawer is still full of the now wrinkled pages from these French interventions, which Molnar had sent me with his "*hommages cordiaux.*" Despite my own affinity for the late-medieval and early-modern objects of his scorn, including Ockham, Luther, and Calvin, it always seemed best that I should not push him too hard on this subject. I did agree with most of his political judgments, and besides, I found no compelling reason to argue over what appeared to be relatively antiquarian matters. I incline toward an idealist reformulation of what Neo-Thomists define as the realist position (holding to something that Molnar would reject as a Kantian adulteration of true epistemology). Nonetheless, unlike him I have never believed that the academic vulgarities of our age stem from a rejection of medieval realism. Too many intervening things had to occur before one could move from doubting the existence of universals to Richard Rorty and Jürgen Habermas, to name just two particularly outspoken representatives of the multicultural imperative.

What got me interested in Molnar's work and what finally led to our meeting was a book he published about thirty years ago, *Le socialisme sans visage* (1976). In it Molnar outlined a political paradigm that he thought was emerging in the Third World. It combined military dictatorship with a planned economy, and while Westerners might compare it to interwar European fascism, the result was considerably different. Unlike European fascist regimes, Third World dictatorships had no frustrated or intimidated bourgeoisie from whom they could draw support; they also had to deal in most cases with an inchoate national sense among tribal populations that had never developed into nation-states and had never developed the characteristically fascist cult of the leader, beyond a succession of rotating strongmen. Although the argument in *Le socialisme sans visage* is brilliantly made, it turned out to have only limited applicability to a steadily changing world. The *Tiers Monde*, about which many Europeans speak as if it were truly unified, is too heterogeneous to permit the sweeping generalizations that Molnar draws in his monograph. Moreover, much of the non-Western world has fallen into the kind of thugocracy that the late Peter Bauer (another native of Budapest) depicted in his many books. Governments that function by stealing and eradicating opposition do not stand for a new paradigm. They illustrate the problem that St. Augustine identified as "brigandage," criminal government, which is a very ancient and widespread affliction. But the merit of Molnar's exposition, and certainly the reason it impressed me, was the attempt to explain non-Western dictatorships without engaging in democratic moralizing. As a political observer, far more than as a Catholic apologist, Molnar has dared to think outside the bounds of convention.

In 1982–83, while I was enjoying a Guggenheim Fellowship, preparing *The Search for Historical Meaning*, and editing the mildly conservative historical journal *Continuity* (then subsidized and promoted by ISI), I came to know both Molnar and Lukacs as personal friends and as contributors to my journal. Each provided copy and abundant advice, which I was glad to receive from these esteemed older colleagues. I met Lukacs for the first time at Hillsdale College almost a quarter of a century ago, after having read such well-known works of his as *Historical Consciousness* (1968), *The Passing of the Modern Age* (1970), *The Great Powers & Eastern Europe* (1953), and *A New History of the Cold War* (1966). The time we spent together resulted in a durable friendship that has persisted to the present day. Several times I have invited John to address my students and colleagues at the different institutions where I have taught. Since my move to Lancaster County, Pennsylvania, which is about one hour and fifteen minutes (without speeding) by car from Lukacs's home near Valley Forge, the two of us have periodically gotten together for dinner with our spouses. A shared misfortune is that both of us have been widowed (John has lost two wives). On the brighter side, our present wives get along, while John and I have continued to quarrel in a family way. John has always treated me as a younger brother, and I have argued with him respectfully in a way that befits the relation to which we have grown accustomed.

My wife Mary has always professed great affection for John, whom she characterizes as an Old World gentleman. He dutifully rises at the dinner table whenever a woman sits down or leaves and is thoroughly charming in conversation with the opposite sex, always knowing exactly what to say (or not to say) to each woman whom he meets. It is impossible to make him understand the feminist movement, because John's entire conception of a nonaberrant society assumes the permanence of formerly recognized gender distinctions. He is highly skeptical that such "crazy ideas" can have a long-range effect, or that what today is called multiculturalism can permanently destroy group solidarity, despite the spread of a postbourgeois culture. For John such unsettling social patterns have no real historical significance, as opposed to ethnicity and to what he sees as the coming reaction against globalism.

Over the years John has sent me two kinds of notes, one consisting of green-bordered postcards full of breathlessly rendered news, and the other consisting of much longer letters, covered with dense typing, that take aim at some blunder I have recently committed. The second kind of letter is more personal and also more likely to yield insights—e.g., the voluminous missive that John sent in 1990 which commented on my recently published intellectual biography of Carl Schmitt. It was apparent from this communication that John did not share my admiration for my subject and believed that in the future I should pick thinkers more wisely before embarking on extensive research.

The figure whom John thought I should be treating in a monograph was the Italian sociologist (and Francophone economist) Vilfredo Pareto. Both of us had considerable admiration for Pareto as an analyst of party politics and of the irrational roots of political behavior. John tried to talk me into this project for several years and then began to alternate it with a second one that he thought suited my talents and interests even better: a study of the generation of 1914 that helped to construct interwar ideologies. Unhappily, the UCLA historian Robert Wohl, and others here and in Europe, had already written on the theme that John proposed; and it seemed to me that the only way a biographical study of Pareto would do well in the U.S., given his identification of democracy with rule by self-serving elites, would be as part of an intellectual history of Europe in the early twentieth century. Although I never wrote that history, my enduring interest in Pareto is apparent from my presentation of liberal critiques of modern democracy, particularly in *After Liberalism*. And at least part of John's recommendation that I undertake a period study found its way into his elegantly composed *Budapest 1900* (1988). Although John was gracious enough to blurb *After Liberalism* and *The Conservative Movement*, I have always had the impression that he was showing provisional kindness, to be made full when I made good on those tasks which he had set for me.

John believes that the "establishment" has never recognized his work. He has also dwelled on his longtime poor relations with neoconservatives, of whom he holds a generally low opinion, and he maintains that these problems go back to the time when Sidney Hook and other neoconservatives in reviews of his books asserted that he was an anti-Semite. This accusation, which he has mentioned to our shared friend Lee Congdon as well as to me, has understandably grated on John, who spent the German occupation of Hungary in 1944 hiding from Hitler's Hungarian collaborators with his mother's Jewish parents.

But from what I can tell, John's mistreatment at the hands of his supposed adversaries has been more than balanced by neoconservative praise—for example, in *Commentary*, for *Duel* (1991) and for John's other books about Churchill. In their interpretations of Churchill, Joe McCarthy, and Truman, John and the neoconservatives have been generally on the same page, as can be seen from his recent harsh criticism of Pat Buchanan's assault on the statecraft of Winston Churchill. As far as I can tell, moreover, his works have come out with prestigious presses, and they have elicited kind words from, among many other dignitaries, George Kennan, Jacques Barzun, Lewis Lapham, and George Will. (For many years, he and Kennan, who lived no more than thirty miles away and is the subject of his latest book, were close friends.) John's last few books have catapulted him into widely televised question-and-answer sessions in Borders and in other bookstores in Philadelphia and Washington. While John has never denied the fact of his fame, he still frets over the doubting few who consider his writing to be "less than history." But such detractors are now mostly in their graves, and they are certainly not to be found among the editors of *American Heritage* and other respected historical magazines in which John's essays have appeared.

There are things in John's work that tend to be, as the French might say, *à rebours*, that is, to go against the grain of recent trends in historiography. This remains the case even if he sometimes appears to be following a postmodern trend by challenging the idea of "historical objectivity." In *Historical Consciousness* and at least parenthetically in almost everything else he has written, Lukacs questions the ideal of objectivity that has made the practice of history into a "science." Such a pursuit, he insists, is futile given the fact that "what happens cannot be separated from what people think has happened." Over against historiography as "scientism," Lukacs holds up the "evolving historical consciousness" that has "entered the blood" of the present generation. He views this popular historical sense with more sympathy than the "scientific study of history," which he rejects as an ideal aim. Lukacs holds the view that "certain concepts of teaching professional historiography that were developed during the last two centuries are no longer adequate."

Lest the reader believe that what we are talking about is the abandonment of historical research for improvised narratives about invented pasts, Lukacs does make clear that he is not talking about "subjectivist" standards. Least of all does he exhibit patience for the attempt to guess what might have inwardly motivated historical actors. He tries to focus attention on what historians and their readers can understand, that is, the comprehensible purpose that reveals itself in the remembered and/or reconstructed past. Neither his flattering observations about the historical-mindedness of the rising generation nor his invectives against "scientism" lead him into substituting anecdotes for the historian's craft. In the end, Lukacs introduces nuance into his impassioned case against objective history.

But a second and more telling argument than the war against "scientific history" runs through *Historical Consciousness*, and this may be the stronger part of Lukacs's distilled understanding of "the remembered past." In this meticulously written but largely impressionistic work, which often reads like a series of aphorisms, he tells his reader: "The sentiments and the ideas of peoples remain the main motive force of nations." Furthermore: "National interest like self-interest tends to produce its own rationalization; but national interest like self-interest is produced by sentiments, inclinations, tendencies, and ideas." Lukacs questions (in a way that anticipates my own perception) whether the terms "conservative" and "liberal" describe the politics of the present democratic epoch. This nomenclature, which comes down from the early nineteenth century, belonged to predemocratic states, regimes that did not solicit popular support by redistributing collected wealth. And only before the First World War did these governments make electoral capital by stirring up belligerent national passions. Lukacs's conclusion (which reprises the insight of German historian Friedrich Meinecke) that nationalism and socialism are the "common denominators of all totalitarian regimes" should not surprise us. Such late-modern regimes bring together in a lethal mixture the dominant themes of mass democratic politics.

Lukacs views nationality and ethnicity not only as the staples of democratic politics, and particularly populist movements, but also as the keys for grasping modern history. This focus on the persistence of ethnicity sets Lukacs apart from conventional academic historians, and it may be his boldest and most critical contribution to historical debate. But this position also allows Lukacs to stumble into certain errors, especially when he uses his emphasis on nationality to express his feelings against the Germans and in favor of the British. One glaring instance of this tendency can be found in his *A New History of the Cold War*, in which Lukacs attributes the political positions of Eisenhower's Secretary of State John Foster Dulles to his "racial background." Writes Lukacs: "This Dutch American, an early admirer of the Boers against England, who was unusually sympathetic toward

Germany, brought with him an enduring core of distrust toward England together with the belief that the alliance with Germany must be the cornerstone of American politics."

Much in this characterization is factually questionable, once we move beyond the facts that Dulles was part Dutch and, like Eisenhower, cultivated cordial relations (for excellent geopolitical reasons) with Konrad Adenauer's postwar government in West Germany. Dulles, whom Lukacs tells us correctly was a strict Presbyterian, had for the most part Scottish ancestors. At one time an ardent Wilsonian, Dulles had fervently supported England in World War I, and he later constructed the controversial "war-guilt" clauses that were inserted into the Treaty of Versailles, in which the Germans were forced to accept exclusive guilt for the war just concluded.

Lukacs likewise insists on a decisive link between anticommunist sentiment in the '50s and the German-Americans and other ethnic groups who supposedly fuelled the anticommunist "witch-hunts" of that era. He overlooks the fact that anticommunist and anti-Nazi positions often resided in the same public, one that was equally outraged by the brutal aggressions and mass killing of Hitler and Stalin. And, as Justus Doenecke and Wayne S. Cole both document in their relevant writings, no significant pro-Nazi sentiment can be located among those who in 1940 and 1941 opposed America's entry into the Second World War. Even less demonstrable, if not entirely nonexistent, were the Anglophobe German Americans and Irish Americans in whom Lukacs discerns pro-Nazi anticommunist sentiments: allegedly these types came into their own during the Eisenhower administration.

Such blanket charges have helped endear Lukacs (a situation that he would certainly not welcome) to some spokesmen of the anti-anticommunist Left. I learned about his statements on Dulles from a colleague in the history department at Rockford College, one who invariably took the Soviet side during the Cold War. In light of the passages in question, my colleague advanced his flattering opinion that Lukacs "really understood Dulles." My reaction to this praise given for bad reasons was less than enthusiastic.

Lukacs's anti-Teutonic and anti-anticommunist remarks are the least defensible aspect of his historical worldview, which is neither leftist nor particularly fashionable. From *The Great Powers & Eastern Europe* to *Democracy and Populism* (2005), Lukacs has treated national and ethnic sentiments as being of the first order of importance for interpreting the present age. This position offers a challenge to those who would reduce social and political phenomena to material needs or to the effects of material oppression. But here too Lukacs may sometimes push a good thing too far, e.g., when he underestimates the appeal of Communist ideals or overrates the continued attraction of fascism, which he equates with popular government reflecting strong nationalist passions. Unlike the Left, which extols communism at least in theory, Lukacs considers the Marxist worldview extraneous to what moves the masses of humanity. He has said repeatedly that "the real prophet of the twentieth century was Mussolini rather than Lenin," who shortsightedly identified revolution with internationalism. What made communism work in practice, to whatever extent it did, was its leaders' shrewd incorporation of national movements into their globalist ideology. John believes that what the internationalist Left professes is nonetheless pie in the sky, and as far as he sees, the unchanging bull in the china shop, whatever it calls itself, is the nationalist Right. He ascribes a hidden right-wing gestalt to what allowed both communism and the Soviet empire, aside from brute force, to endure for decades. The Communists energized and befriended "workers' nations" and were therefore able to move beyond Marxist abstractions toward a policy of national solidarity.

The author's parents
Andrew and Ruth Gottfried,
Coney Island, New York
1939

Paul with his father Andrew at Pleasure Beach
Bridgeport, Connecticut 1944

Left, Paul with Maternal Grandmother, Spring 1942
Right, Paul and Dennis Gottfried, October 1954

Paul, his father Andrew, and brother Dennis in front of the Statehouse in Hartford, Connecticut, 1958

The author, Paul Gottfried
Cleveland, Ohio
1968

Paul's youngest daughter, Sara with his mother, Ruth Gottfried
Bethesda, Maryland 1986

Sara with Murray
Elizabethtown, 2002

Gottfried Family, 1978
(from left, Paul's father-in-law, Barbara, Paul, Beth, Dana, Jonathan, and Joe)

Eldest Grandson, Joshua
2006

Grandson, Raffi
2007

Granddaughter, Ruthie
2008

The author, his wife Mary, and Murray

photo courtesy of Elizabethtown College, 2004

"American Gothic Gottfrieds"

photo by Grant Havers

Gary Ulmen and Paul Piccone
New York, 1990

Standing, from left, Paul Gottfried, Sam Francis, Michael Warder, Lew Rockwell, Peter Stanlis, Joe Sobran, Tom Fleming, and David Gordon. Seated, from left, George Resch, Allan Carlson, Barton Blumert, Jeff Tucker, and Chronicles Associate Editor, Kate Dalton.
Rockford, Illinois, 1987

With Thomas Molnar and
Tomislav Sunic, 1989

With Peter Stanlis
2008

With Richard Nixon, 1992
photo by Forrest MacDonald

My own view in this matter is exactly the opposite of John's. As far as I can see, it is the Left, given its reformulation of Christian universalism and the Christian commitment to comforting the oppressed, which has produced the greater danger to Western civilization. The Left projects a fantasy that fits the Western moral imagination. It thrives as a "Christian heresy," according to Karl Barth, a brilliant Christian theologian who himself succumbed to that heresy. A Christian civilization created the moral and eschatological framework that leftist anti-Christians have taken over and adapted. It is the fascists, not the Communists or multiculturalists, who were the sideshow in modern Western history. As the anthropologist Mircea Eliade observed fifty years ago, fascism, and in particular its most violent and aberrant form, German Nazism, bungled the task of fitting established Christian societies into a revamped heathen or pagan mythology.

Eliade expressed concern that the Left's use of Christian mythology made it unstoppable, barring a successful reappropriation by Christianity of its own redemptive history. While there were intellectual efforts in the nineteenth and early twentieth centuries to move in a neopagan direction, fascist leaders could not effect the change of mind that was necessary for their triumph. Fascist, and especially Nazi, politics aroused indignation in a way that the Communists did not. The reason was certainly not that Communist regimes in practice were less brutal. It was, rather, as Eliade points out, that they adapted Christian rhetoric and Christian values to justify their murderous social experiments. Communist states profited from two ingrained beliefs that were linked to Christianity directly or indirectly: the Christian vision of a final universal justice for the unjustly suffering, and the Enlightenment's recasting of this vision as scientific progress. Lest there be doubt about where I stand, I agree entirely with Ernst

Nolte, who in 1996, in correspondence with the French historian François Furet, depicted European fascism as "a secondary movement," that is, an ultimately disastrous attempt to subdue the revolutionary Left through an awkward imitation. Nolte has advanced the opinion that everything being equal, the Left has enjoyed a steady recruiting advantage relative to the far Right. It has drawn support by recycling Judeo-Christian ideals and eschat-ology and has done so with brilliant success even while abandoning Marxist baggage.

Having clarified my difference with him, let me also stress that I agree with John that groups are driven by ethnic and national feelings far more than contemporary Americans wish to notice. John is correct that ethnic hostilities often seethe behind the exterior of human-rights language and the rhetoric of inclusiveness. Such assumptions, which have shaped my recent writings, draw heavily on John's understanding of ethnicity in the U.S. John's perceptions here are particularly evident in his treatment of WASP social decline in *Philadelphia 1900–1950: Patricians and Philistines* (1981), *A Thread of Years* (1998), and *Outgrowing Democracy* (1984), and in his wise reminder that ethnic conflict did not end because the old Anglo-Saxon elite has gone into eclipse. The fading of the old guard from prominence and leadership, together with its waning self-respect, has accelerated the venting of hostilities by more demonstrative ethnics who nurse grievances against the old patriciate and against each other.

One of the best treatments of American immigration that I have had the fortune to read is the chapter "The Leap Across the Sea" in Lukacs's *Outgrowing Democracy*. The observations in this work about immigration to the U.S. capture the mixture of relentless self-Americanization and "the more complex psychic process" that have gone into creating "hyphenated Americans." Furthermore: "the American tendency (or, rather, wish) to believe that a man was newly born when he arrived in America, the land of freedom, became a piece of furniture in the minds of millions of immigrants." But this tendency almost always conflicted with the reality that the new and old Americans lived in different worlds, and one consequence of this separation, according to Lukacs, is that even the best of Americanized immigrant writers have either told their own ethnic stories or created implausible and ultimately parochial pictures of their Americanization. An illustration of these limits for Lukacs (as he pointed out in an essay in the Fall–Winter 1976 issue of *Salmagundi*) is the "movie-historical confection *Ragtime*" in which the politically engaged novelist E. L. Doctorow tries to offer a panorama of social life in the U.S. in the early twentieth century. Contrary to his intention but perhaps inevitably, Lukacs explains, Doctorow's "description of the Jewish immigrant family is fairly telling while his description of the older American family consists of cardboard figures."

Lukacs relates how his students at Chestnut Hill believed accounts about how their families got here from some mysterious place in Europe. In all such narrative exercises there prevails the same fiction: the ancestor of the student preparing the essay "began [his life] in America, not earlier." When the student does get around to an earlier, pre-American family life, "these facts are mythical, insubstantial, irrelevant." Since Lukacs's impressions reach back twenty-five to thirty years, it may be useful to add here my own painfully accumulated impressions of the apparently forgotten ethnicity of my students. Ethnic and denominational differences do not exist for them, at least not on the surface. It is considered downright gauche to mention such differences, except while dwelling on the suffering of blacks and other authorized victim groups or on the bigotry of whites, particularly those who bear the stigma of residing in the American South.

In my senior class in political science, most of my students' opinions about electoral behavior echo Anthony Downs's *Economic Theory of Democracy* (1957). A work full of microeconomic terminology, this treatise ascribes voting preferences to aggregate perceptions about material interest. Downs's questionable interpretation of voting behavior, which benefits from the consumerism of his readers more than from the author's fondness for government planning, presents voters as financially driven, self-interested individuals. When I ask students whether other variables might explain what is being investigated, and when I dare to point out that white Protestants are predominantly Republicans and that white ethnic Catholics, Jews, and blacks are by and large Democrats, the students typically stare at me in disbelief. This is not the explanation which professors are supposed to give, unless it is to stress that Republicans are "non-inclusive," which is certainly not my intent. In fact, when students lay the charge of "noninclusiveness" at the doorstep of Republicans, I retort that there are no critical differences in the way the two parties "reach out" to minorities. The Republicans assume their WASP base and then expend considerable energy trying to raid the votes on the other side. Being a Republican or being a Democrat is mostly about ethnic self-identification, as is obviously the case in the South, where whites and blacks have exchanged party affiliations but continue to identify with opposing parties. Pointing out the persistence of ethnic antagonism seems to my students "un-American," although few of them have reflected on my arguments. Admitting the possibility of my hypothesis does not square with the Americanization process that our students' ancestors underwent in the uncertain past. It occasions questions about the operation of old and sometimes misplaced resentments that continue to affect American voting behavior.

Although *Outgrowing Democracy*, which John sent me as a gift, has not sold as well as many of John's other books, it has won my respect because of its sterling honesty. It seems doubtful that Doubleday would have published such a book in the mid-'80s by a less established author who was equally indifferent to political propriety. Whether stressing the democracy deficit, exploring the Americanizing process, or expressing skeptical attitudes about racial harmony, Lukacs avoids unseemly optimism in his original construction of a "history of the United States in the twentieth century."

His book illustrates John's Old World manner of observing what is around him and then articulating these observations while being guided by an uncorrupted sense of judgment. His comments about blacks and whites clashing in the late '60s recall those of my father, who viewed them with the same grim resignation as the inescapable consequence of trying to bring together vastly different groups as equals. My father would have recognized his own thought in Lukacs's opinion that Americans were wrong to think that racial harmony could be achieved by having the Supreme Court declare segregation unconstitutional "on the basis of arguments drawn from the abstractions of sociology." Such reasoning, according to Lukacs, changed little sociologically: "The association of whites and blacks in many occupations and at certain levels increased," while "a cruel and crude savagery," "reminiscent of the Third World," swept through American cities. Thus Lukacs soberly concludes his reflections on race relations in the U.S. circa 1980.

In a long German letter dated May 16, 1998, which my wife inserted into a folder next to a note from Caroline Nisbet, the gracious widow of Robert Nisbet, Erik von Kuehnelt-Leddihn offers this comment about my reference (in an earlier letter) to the then newly formed Historical Society: "There are few Catholics associated with it." But Erik was happy to see among the names of the founding members that of John Lukacs, "whom I brought to Chestnut Hill." My Austrian correspondent still obviously valued John's friendship, a sentiment that he knew I fully shared. Unbeknownst to Erik at the time, however, was that I had tried to find a post at the school where he and John had earlier taught—and whence John had recently retired. In the late '80s I had been casting about for an academic position while working in Washington as a senior editor for *The World and I*. John proposed the idea of approaching his administration about hiring me for his soon-to-be-vacated position, which he rightly understood would be a hard task, given his institution's financial constraints. Although this plan went nowhere, it still amuses me to think that I might have been the most recent link in the line of maverick Central European thinkers who had graced Chestnut Hill's history department.

This counterfactual scenario comes to mind partly because of the practice my wife and I have adopted of late, which is to hike along the Wissahickon River near that small Catholic girls' college where I had hoped to teach. The trail along this river, which originates near the college and empties into the Schuylkill in North Philadelphia, is among the most scenic I have found in any American urban area. By following Germantown Road past the Morris Arboretum, past the college's neo-Gothic architecture, and then across the bridge spanning the trickle whence the Wissahickon meanders southward, one eventually arrives at the village of Chestnut Hill, a settlement that should be familiar to readers of Lukacs's vignettes of Philadelphia patricians. There the cobblestone streets, funky shops, stone houses, and lime-washed churches emit such charm that I find myself answering "Chestnut Hill" whenever the question arises where we should go on a leisurely Sunday afternoon. I have gone to the park adjoining the village for hikes with my daughter, son-in-law, and grandchildren, when they come from Central New Jersey. And as I walk with them along the trail and through the village, I think of the now lost possibility of having gone to Chestnut Hill to live and work. Such might have happened.

Although I had profited from his commentaries in *National Review* and, even earlier, from his tract *Freiheit oder Gleichheit* (1953), I did not meet Erik until 1989, when Claes Ryn invited me to hear him lecture at Catholic University. Afterwards we dined at a small Irish pub near Michigan Avenue, where I continued to be struck by our speaker's talents and uncommon erudition. He was plainly fluent in several languages, and during his lecture he had quoted by heart entire sections from the Gospel of John in Greek, followed by long citations from Genesis in Hebrew. As someone who had studied these texts in the original languages, I was astonished by Erik's power of recall, as I later was by the knowledge he demonstrated of comparative linguistic morphologies when our talk turned to Far Eastern languages. At dinner he showed me his sketches of his grandson, all of which revealed fine workmanship. He then explained that since he had left his last academic post in the U.S., he had made his living as an artist, author, and lecturer. In addition, he had published several novels, two of which I subsequently found in English translation. Since the mid-'50s, however, he had limited himself to political writings in English and German.

From Erik's descriptions of his academic adventures at Saint Peter's in Jersey City, at Georgetown, at Fordham, and finally at Chestnut Hill, it was apparent that he had found his colleagues odd ducks. He was used to living in a "sociologically Catholic" society, like the Tyrol, but he thought American Catholics less likeable. In the U.S., he noted in a way that recalled Lukacs's observation on this subject, his colleagues and their families tried too hard to be culturally American. The result, particularly among the Irish, was a grim Catholic ritualism combined with an often defensive Americanism. Erik also expressed wonder that Protestants here and elsewhere persisted in thinking of Luther as "*der Urheber der Moderne* [the creator of modernity]," when in fact he was a profoundly reactionary medieval monk who would have been repulsed by the modern world. Erik's suspicion of Protestant cultures, a recurrent theme in his work, did not pertain to the original Protestant theology, which he interpreted as authentically Christian. What he found amiss about the Protestants is the reckless fashion in which they embraced the Enlightenment, which, according to one of his letters, "has its origins in a second-class version of the Renaissance." The break that occurred with the Reformation had removed a check on the drift toward the democratic and social-engineering Left; nonetheless, the same cultural forces, remarked Erik, are now permeating Catholic Europe and wreaking havoc there as well.

I am still not entirely sure why I received two long letters from Erik, both in 1998. The closest I can come to an explanation is that the author was responding to the galleys of *After Liberalism*, which I may have sent him; he also refers to certain letters of mine (of which I have no extant copies) in which I discuss his definitions of Right, Left, conservative, and liberal. What struck me about these missives is that they came from a man who was then approaching ninety but could still present his ideas in elegant German. They reflected his passionate engagement in the kind of debates that he had been pursuing for more than fifty years.

From his comments it is evident that he and I disagreed about certain subjects. The reason for my dissent goes back to *Leftism: From*

Sade and Marx to Hitler and Marcuse, an English-language book originally published in 1974 and then republished with a preface by William F. Buckley Jr. in 1990. In the new edition Pol Pot had replaced Marcuse, perhaps as a concession to political currency. I did not accept Erik's view, which was once fashionable on the American Right, that all odious mass killers in the twentieth century can be placed at the doorstep of the historic Left. After all, there were right-wing killers, especially in the interwar period, who appealed to the fear of the revolutionary Left in order to brutalize entire countries. Although admittedly such tyrants were fewer than their leftist counterparts, and although (particularly in Hitler's case) they often borrowed freely from the Soviet experiment, I saw no purpose in calling every morally objectionable politician a leftist. I also disagreed with Erik's practice of pinning a "democratic" label on every modern totalitarian. Although, like him, I have come to shudder at certain god terms and hold no brief for democratic idolatry, clearly not all modern tyrants have been "democrats." A label that could be made to apply equally to the Nazis and to social-democratic regimes seemed imprecise and free-floating. Such linguistic self-indulgence reminded me of the practice of making "conservative" synonymous with whatever the American center-left used to espouse but eventually repudiated. This category includes everything from "moderate" feminism to the 1964 Civil Rights Act. I bring up this objection because Erik rightly complained about the indiscriminate use to which the "conservative" label had been applied in American politics.

Erik responded by pointing to the huge overlap between the Nazis and earlier revolutionary regimes that had called themselves "democratic," from the French Jacobins onward. From administrative centralization to the mass extermination of political enemies, such governments had more in common with each other than they did with nontotalitarian regimes. On the opposite side from these totalitarian democrats, in Erik's scheme of things, were decent governments such as authentically conservative ones, which can "no longer exist since there is nothing enduring that is left to defend," or else liberal regimes that subordinate democratic equality to constitutional liberties. Erik identified America's founders with an antidemocratic liberal tradition, and he insisted that such right-thinking gentlemen as Hamilton and Adams could have nothing in common with the kind of democratic power-grabbing that has become an increasing problem since the French Revolution.

Although one might accuse him of playing fast and loose with his terms, Erik had a valid point, even if he pushed it too hard. Democracy and liberalism do lead in different directions as historical phenomena; *After Liberalism* stresses the tension between these forces and explains why democratic equality has proved stronger than those constitutional limits intended to contain it. Furthermore, administrative overreach is no mere excrescence in our evolving democracy, as American Republicans would like us to believe. It is something essential to the democratic project of finding new intrusive ways to implement our evolving understanding of equality. Above all, I respected Erik's oft-made declaration that he was "a liberal" who respected the "early liberals," to the extent that they were not motivated by anticlericalism and other fanaticisms of the French Revolution. Neither Erik nor I had any problem with making such a declaration, nor with recognizing what Erik described as the "dirty, putrid fungus that one calls 'liberal' in the U.S.," which is "characteristic of the semantic confusion of which America is rich in examples."

In one letter Erik raised an objection to the weird usage of "holocaust," in which a term that denotes a Greek sacrifice is made to refer inappropriately to "genocide." If that usage is meant to underline what is unique about the Nazi slaughter of European Jewry, Erik observed, it involves something of a malapropism. Nor could he understand why the German "*Nahosten* [Near East]" becomes "Middle East," in geographically misleading (American) English. In French the corresponding term is "*Proche Orient*"; nonetheless, in Italian the same region is rendered as "*Medio Oriente*," a designation that is no better than the English term that Erik found typical of American "semantic confusion."

John and Erik both observed the distinctively American approach to terms that recur in discussion but are only vaguely defined. An interest in political semantics, a characteristic quite pronounced in my three subjects, is common to Central Europeans in a way that it is foreign to most Americans. The Americans I have encountered, including journalists and academics, embrace generally unexamined terms in order to designate political phenomena that Europeans until recently have understood differently.

Most political scientists of my acquaintance never seem to ask whether "democracy" can mean anything other than its present American avatar. The term "democratic capitalism," which is bandied about in newspapers, is a kind of filler language. It is based on nothing more than an overgeneralization concerning an accidental and time-bound coexistence between particular economic and governing arrangements. It might be easily discovered that capitalism and political equality can operate and have operated independently of each other in many societies. If a democratic administrative state coupled with a mixed economy is an American preference, then it should be possible to indicate this without imagining it to be a universal good or without conferring on one's contrivance or situation the pompous label "democratic capitalism." And the pairings and correlations involved in this historical phenomenon include tensions, as Kuehnelt-Leddihn pointed out, between the democratic imperative to redistribute and equalize and the exigencies of a free economy.

Yet Americans disregard their unreflective political semantics while proclaiming that they have charted a unique path to political salvation. Not surprisingly, these persistent practices and parochial habits have had significance beyond our borders, a point that I have made to a generally unreceptive public in my recent books. Because of America's cultural reach, we have passed on to others our political semantics and their underlying prejudices, along with such other made-in-America artifacts as rap and Kraft food products. The questioning of those political concepts which are taken for granted on this side of the Atlantic has driven my scholarship—perhaps more so than good sense or professional interest would warrant.

My Central European mentality has played a critical role here. And the colorful subjects of this chapter foreshadowed and influenced my own acquired tendency to ask questions in a way that is not thoroughly American. Kuehnelt-Leddhin and Molnar, at least, have gone beyond an immanentist argument against "democratic equality" to challenge the egalitarian project in a more general manner. Their position has not been the usual leftist one—namely, that equality is the essence of democracy but alas we have not worked at it hard enough. Rather, they have said exactly the opposite: that once a people or their administrative and judicial elite start along the path to ever greater equality, there is simply no way to stop the process. Democratic equality is an Aristotelian excess writ large over an entire society, and it keeps spilling over into social relations until it has infected everything. Through their ceaseless and not always respectful probing, my subjects have called attention to what might otherwise have gone unnoticed amid the boisterous celebrations of American democracy and equality.

VII

Two Pugnacious Republicans

On a blustery March morning in 1992 I found myself standing in front of the eighteenth-century pile on Third Street in Philadelphia that had once housed the First Bank of the United States. At 11:00 A.M., Pat Buchanan (1938–), who was then seeking the presidential nomination of his party against a faltering President George H. W. Bush, stood atop the stairs and made a pitch for Republican votes in Pennsylvania. Fresh from his unexpected victory in the New Hampshire primary, Buchanan was still a presidential hopeful. His hope, however, would soon be dashed by circumstances that were becoming evident by the time of his arrival in Philadelphia.

Buchanan's deteriorating relations with the neoconservatives, and more generally with the Jewish liberal establishment, and his fragile state organizations, which were functioning on a shoestring with the help of unpaid volunteers, revealed his campaign's vulnerability. Although the sitting president was an embarrassingly inept speaker who had angered his base, Buchanan was in no position to take away the prize. The most he could hope to achieve was to cause headaches in the White House, which he managed to do for a few months before he went into a tailspin by the end of the spring.

Buchanan's brief appearance in Philadelphia was all he could offer of himself to his well-wishers in Pennsylvania. But it may indicate something about his popularity that Pat pulled as much as one-quarter of the state's primary vote without even the semblance of a professional staff. (I and a former congressman from Pittsburgh helped steer what there was of a largely spontaneous state campaign.)

The fate of Buchanan as a gutsy spoiler who could never quite make it as a national political figure recalls the plight of Hannibal, the Carthaginian commander who overran Italy with his Celtic and North African armies. Despite his strategic abilities and his stunning success on the battlefield, Hannibal never gained the support of Rome's Italian allies. His military boldness did not bring him victory over the Roman Republic, the goal he had imagined to be in his grasp during the Second Punic War, particularly after he had wiped out the Roman Legions at the Battle of Cannae in 216 B.C. Buchanan likewise mounted impressive campaigns without being able to carry them to successful completion. Like Hannibal, he was unable to peel away the enemy's allies. The party professionals and the inveterate Republican voters stayed with the incumbent president, and where Buchanan did best was in attracting blue-collar Democrats in open primaries.

After he had finished speaking in Philadelphia, I joined Pat and his wife for lunch in a nearby hotel. The first question he asked me as we walked among the Secret Service agents who had recently been assigned to him was "what does the chief think about what I am doing?" He thereupon answered his question by responding with a sheepish grin: "He probably thinks I shouldn't be in this." The reference was to former president Richard Nixon, whom I had visited the preceding week. Nixon had indeed stressed that "Pat should get out," but he also explained that he was following his "party's interests" out of mere habit. He also opined that "Pat has lots of guts."

Nixon had nothing flattering to say about President Bush. Buchanan had worked on Nixon's staff for almost nine years, from January 1966 until Nixon's resignation as president in August 1974, and throughout this period the two had gotten along well. Their views about student radicals had dovetailed, and if Pat made any mistake in advising Nixon on how to deal with the media, it was pushing his chief toward a starkly confrontational style. In Nixon's case that was clearly a bad call, given his proverbial quarrels with liberal journalists and his inability to disguise his animosity toward familiar foes. Pat was correct when he pointed out in *Right from the Beginning* (1988) that Nixon was a stunning conversationalist: "To anyone who has gone through it, a conversation with Richard Nixon could be an exhilarating and exhausting experience." But his mental acuity and wit were not the qualities that came through in his battles with the press; and going to war against his presumed and for the most part real adversaries did not enhance Nixon's reputation, a fact that was evident well before the revelations that followed the Watergate break-in.

Still, there was something about Pat's loyalty to persons and unvarnished patriotism that Nixon fully admired, and I've no doubt that he would have supported his presidential bid, whether or not there was a sitting Republican president, if Nixon thought that his campaign had a future. The former president never revealed any personal affection for Bush or his family, and he stressed the fact that his endorsement was a matter of professional courtesy. I am therefore not surprised that one of Nixon's courtiers, Kevin Phillips, has produced a vitriolic biography of the Bushes and their plutocratic connections. Unlike the former president, when I met him Phillips was openly contemptuous of his future subjects and expressed that attitude in Nixon's presence. His host did not contradict him.

As I sat with Pat and his wife Shelley at what turned out to be a private luncheon (which included a former student of mine turned banker), it was evident that Pat thought that he had a chance to oust the incumbent president. According to his analysis, voters were tired of professional politicians, workers were concerned with protecting their jobs against Asian countries that were dumping cheap goods in order to capture American markets, and unrestricted immigration was creating havoc. Above all, the cultural and moral advances that had been made by what was once called the "counterculture" were arousing a strong reaction, and Pat believed that his candidacy gave voice to these social concerns. Even though his organization was a hand-to-mouth affair, when it came to the issues he was striking a chord. Or so he thought.

Our friendship went back to the late '80s, when I began to receive notes and inscribed copies of his publications from Pat's hand. My review, written in 1988, of his autobiographical *Right from the Beginning* for *The World and I* elicited an enthusiastic acknowledgment, one that arrived like a bolt out of the blue in my mailbox. The review reflected a new direction in my thinking, and it offered a comparative study of Buchanan the warrior and William F. Buckley Jr., who was depicted in my review as perpetually temporizing. A then recent biography of Buckley by his leftist admirer John Judis provided the occasion for my parallel lives sketch, in which Buchanan was assigned the higher moral position, despite my scattered references to his rashness. A stream of letters, punctuated by phone calls, commenced between us. When I was preparing the second, expanded edition of *The Conservative Movement*, I sent Pat a particularly juicy chapter on the sources of neoconservative funding. Since he was then already engaged in heated exchanges with some of my subjects, he recycled my revelations, which came out as a controversial syndicated column.

The one phrase I recall from that column was Pat's impassioned call to remove "the neoconservative fleas from the conservative dog." I told him that such a cleansing would not be easy. He retorted that "it would take about six months—not much more." The six months of recovery will soon be twenty years, and the fleas and the dog have become inseparable.

By 1990, Pat was feuding furiously with neoconservative journalists and Zionist lobbyists, starting with Abe Rosenthal of the *New York Times*, Abe Foxman of the Anti-Defamation League, and the entire staff of *Commentary* magazine. At issue were Pat's changing positions on Middle Eastern affairs, in which he went from an exuberant advocate of the Israeli Right to an embattled spokesman for the Palestinians and an unsparing critic of AIPAC. This was followed by a scathing exchange between Buchanan and Rosenthal over the establishment of a Polish Carmelite convent on the grounds of the former concentration camp at Auschwitz. The issues were not quite as one-sided as I might have made them appear in my defenses of Pat. Unlike him, I have never changed my sympathetic position toward the beleaguered plight of the Israelis, even while lamenting the boorishness of Zionist advocates in the U.S. The problem was that the attacks on him were indefensibly extreme, particularly the charge hurled by Rosenthal in 1990 that Buchanan was reviving "medieval blood libels" against the Jews by raising the question of "dual loyalty" against his neoconservative foes. Even more hysterical were the invectives directed against Pat when he challenged the accusation by Rosenthal and Foxman that the Catholic Church and the Polish people had no right to pray for the souls of those exterminated at Auschwitz, because both were accomplices in the Holocaust. Millions of Polish Catholics, including their clergy, as well as European Jews had been killed on the Auschwitz site. Since my late mother-in-law, a Polish Catholic, had shielded Jews from the Nazis at the risk of her life, I was particularly incensed by this stupid libel when I saw it in print.

Yet Pat rushed to assail too many powerful enemies at the same time. This mistake was exemplified by his defense of Ivan Demjanjuk, the Ukrainian immigrant then residing in the U.S. who had been charged by Nazi-hunters with having served as a murderous guard in a Nazi concentration camp. Although the accused immigrant was not the grim figure "Ivan the Terrible" whom the Israelis were looking for (in fact, the Israelis graciously let the suspect off the hook), Demjanjuk may well have been implicated in Nazi crimes, a supposition that was then being explored. It would have been best if Pat had abandoned the issue to other journalists, instead of trying to show that his enemies were far from fair-minded while in pursuit of their targets. Discretion was urgently needed, particularly since Pat may have been planning to run for president at the time that he was rallying to Demjanjuk's defense. Having neoconservative and Jewish liberal enemies can be for an ordinary politician unpleasant; for a presidential candidate of the Old Right, such combined animosity is a truly insurmountable obstacle. Pat's sister Bay, who has worked faithfully for her brother over the years, has often dragged him away from fights, and for those of us who recall Pat's acerbic quarrels of almost twenty years ago, her caution is fully understandable. Like Bay, I too have noted Pat's tendency to move from boldness into rashness, a quality of character that is one of Aristotle's vices.

Having offered this censure, I must also stress that Pat's audacity might be his most attractive quality. When movement conservatives in the 1980s were stampeding into the neoconservative camp for professional and social reasons, Pat refused to go along. Like the father of the German historian Joachim Fest, who lost his teaching position in Berlin for having refused to join the Nazi Party, Pat was the kind of person who would have also responded *"alle aber ich nicht* [everyone but not I]" if asked to go along with something he disapproved of. Murray Rothbard and I would sometimes speculate on why our friend was so ornery, an attribute that we respected, even though we sometimes disagreed with Pat's stated positions. Murray's view, which he expressed in published polemics, is that Pat had had it up to his ears with the "smearbund," those who wielded the "anti-Semitic branding iron" every time they faced an opinion they found unacceptable. He had no doubt that Pat would have been in even deeper trouble in Europe, where a combination of "antifascist" witch-hunting and multicultural indoctrination had already taken hold.

Although I did not disagree with Murray's interpretation, there was something more primal about Pat's reaction to character-assassinating critics. He emphatically believes that while contentiousness may be essential to a free society, there should be fair play in the way argument takes place. Unlike the current European advocates of "tolerance," who seek to throw their opponents into jail as "fascists," Pat accepts the premise that debates should be won or lost on the merits of what is said or proved. It is not a refutation but a slander, albeit one that pretends to hold the moral high ground, to claim, as was once said about me in *Commentary*, that the speaker "should have no place in civil discourse" or that someone who ascribes to neoconservatives dual loyalty is committing "a blood libel against Jews." In my view, Pat considered his detractors bullies who would not debate according to a gentlemanly code, and he therefore went after them with unconcealed anger. And he struck out against them while other self-declared conservatives were knuckling under. By contrast, Pat responded in a manly and principled fashion, even if his rhetoric was not always carefully chosen.

Pat has not turned over a new leaf entirely since his wars of the late '80s and early '90s. In a stream of best-selling books, he has argued passionately for immigration restrictions. In *State of Emergency* (2006), he quotes in profusion the warnings of an even more controversial man of the right, Sam Francis, on the growing dangers of cultural and demographic suicide in the West. Even more audaciously, Pat cites the speech in defense of Western ethnicities that caused Sam to lose his position at the *Washington Times*. The citation may have been intended as a judgment about Sam's seriousness as a thinker—and it might have been meant also as an attempt to needle Sam's neoconservative detractors.

At the Republican National Convention in August 1992, at which Buchanan was allowed to speak by the triumphant Bush team, he mocked the "San Francisco Democrats." The speech was aimed not only at the opposing party, which had just held its convention in San Francisco, but also at the lifestyle liberals, particularly gays, whom Buchanan associated with their Democratic sponsors. Although former president Clinton in his autobiography noted the possible strategic value to Republicans of Buchanan's strictures, his remarks nonetheless evoked a storm of criticism. Not surprisingly, the neoconservatives, who well into the 1980s had inveighed against the gay-liberation movement while presenting homosexuality as a mental disorder, joined the chorus of those who seemed shocked by Pat's speech. From the *New York Times* and *Washington Post* to the *Wall Street Journal*, Buchanan was declared to be an insensitive divider.

The next year, when Pat and Bay launched The American Cause, they decided to pursue a less divisive course. The organization's first conference, held in downtown Washington, was a model of outreach. It featured Michael Medved, a modern Orthodox Jewish movie critic of Hollywood's war on morality: a black woman who was a former welfare mother married to a much older Episcopal priest; and other speakers who might have been chosen for the purpose of counteracting Pat's image as a right-wing bigot. Sam Francis and my late wife sat with me at that conference, to which I had been invited as a discussant. Sam grumbled the entire day about Pat's newly discovered inclusiveness, an acquired quality that he attributed to the shell-shocked state of his friend. "I bet they'll eat this up at the [neoconservative] *Washington Times*," was Sam's comment. He was right. The report on Pat's conference in Sam's old paper was uniformly enthusiastic, despite the previously frenetic efforts of its editorial-page writers to push Pat out of the presidential race.

Once fortified with the sense that he was getting good press, Pat called a second conference, which dealt mostly with culture but also featured me as a keynote speaker on "The New Conservatism." From his note, it seemed that I would be allowed to have my day in the sun. And afterwards, in a long letter dated November 19, 1993, Pat thanked me for my address and announced that "I think we've got them scared." The ones whom we apparently had on the run were the regular Republicans, liberal establishment journalists typified by David Broder, and the hated neocons.

Despite this upbeat letter and a similar one from Bay, I have always thought that I failed miserably as the principal speaker at the conference. This was not because the *Washington Times* and other newspapers predictably ignored my remarks in their reports. More upsetting was the fact that I knew that I had wandered on too long. Many of my allusions to political theory drew blank stares from my listeners. In a labored effort to go along with the prescribed tone, I made it appear that Pat's side would soon triumph. But I did not believe my message, and my attempt to sound exultant and to pretend that our rivals were about to vanish from the historical stage did not have the ring of deep conviction. Never again would I be asked to serve as a keynote speaker. In 2006, when the political theorist Claes Ryn and I were planning the first gathering of a new scholarly organization, the Academy of Philosophy and Letters, the question of a keynote speaker came up. I was delighted that my name was not even considered. As we were laying the groundwork for a plenary gathering in June 2007, I proposed that we bring in Pat Buchanan as our keynoter. Unfortunately, he could not come. But I know that he would have risen to the occasion better than I had done in 1993.

The expanded edition of *The Conservative Movement*, which was published in January 1993, includes a generous blurb from Pat as well as one from his old boss Richard Nixon (1913–94). I had come to know the former president in the late '80s, at about the same time that I was developing a friendship with Pat. While the latter praised me on the dust jacket as the most "skilled pathologist" of our "troubled movement," Nixon, who never imagined himself to be a movement conservative, noted my "brilliant analysis of the situation that affects not only the Right, but all of America." I first made contact with Nixon after the publication of my book *The Search for Historical Meaning*, which was released in 1986 by Northern Illinois University Press. Although I had written this lament on the loss of historical consciousness on the American Right with a Guggenheim Fellowship, I did not expect my ruminations to reach very far. The book had been printed in a run of fifteen hundred copies, which I assumed would be purchased for the most part by university libraries. But the text did unexpectedly well. It was widely reviewed, and it received pages of praise from, among many others, Robert Nisbet. A copy also fatefully landed in the hands of Richard Nixon, who was then doing research for a work on foreign relations that grew into his *1999: Victory Without War* (1988). The former president had quoted me in his work, and he had also indicated in the *American Spectator* (1987) that mine was the most important book he had read in the previous year. As I have since learned, that same volume is prominently displayed in the Richard Nixon Library in Yorba Linda on the former president's office desk, just as it appeared on the day of his death.

Building on this introduction of sorts, I contacted Nixon by letter in his office suite in Woodcliff Lake, New Jersey, in November 1988. I obtained his address from my immediate superior at the time, Professor Morton Kaplan, who had hired me as the senior editor of *The World and I*. Morton had been one of Nixon's advisors on disarmament negotiations with the Soviets, and he was hoping that any friendship I might strike up with his old boss would redound to the benefit of his publication. "Perhaps we can get him to write something for us," was the hope that Morton expressed when he offered to pay my fare from Washington to northern New Jersey if the former president invited me for a visit. In my letter, I dwelled on the fact that my family had voted for him. Indeed, I explained, if I had been twenty-one in 1960, or if the voting age had then been lowered to eighteen, I too would have cast my ballot for him against his Democratic opponent. Within a few days I received a response. Nixon noted that we had had to wait another twelve years, until his presidency, before the voting age was lowered. He also suggested that if I came to the New York area, he would "welcome the opportunity to have a visit." Perhaps to make sure I did come, he provided the telephone number of his secretary, Kathy O'Connor, who would be waiting for my call.

A few weeks later, in early January 1989, I appeared in his office on Chestnut Ridge Road in Woodcliff Lake, and except for a secretary and a Secret Service officer, the two of us seemed entirely alone in his suite of offices, which was situated in an inconspicuous commercial building. Our conversation lasted more than two hours, and there were three things about my host which struck me with particular force. He looked considerably older than he had during his presidency fifteen years earlier. His face was more furrowed; and his strangely curved nose, which the caricaturist Herblock had depicted with malicious glee, was more bent than it had seemed on television when he was president. Nixon had turned seventy-six on the day of my visit; he quipped that "I'm trying to forget my birthday and hope that others will do the same." The president was also remarkably knowledgeable about political theory; he spoke to me about Hegel and Hobbes with genuine enthusiasm and a wealth of facts. He explained that he had studied these thinkers under the influence of his favorite law professor at Duke University, Lon Fuller, the figure to whom he had dedicated his book *1999*.

Another noteworthy quality was his disarmingly personal conversational style. There was nothing in the former president's demeanor that suggested the stiffness of his public persona, particularly as that persona had projected itself after the media went into a feeding frenzy over the Watergate break-in. Unlike the grim, verbally inept politician I had seen under attack, the private Nixon was effusive, eloquent, and entirely affable. There was nothing in our relation even from the start that would indicate the obvious social distance that separated us. The fact that he sent me home with a copy of his newest book containing the flattering inscription "with great respect, to someone who knows the real world," only enhanced my affection for him. He also inscribed a second gift copy—this one for my eldest daughter, Barbara—which provided me with an additional reason to recall my visit with satisfaction.

In my penultimate appearance in *National Review* (July 14, 1989), I wrote a detailed account of my first meeting with the former president, "Nixon Visited and Revisited," in which I dwelled on the two levels on which he appeared to function. On one level, he tried desperately to ingratiate himself with his leftist critics by giving them what he thought they desired—namely, leftist platitudes and left-of-center social policies. He was, after all, identified forever in their minds with the anticommunist politics that propelled him to prominence in California in 1950. Journalists and historians were always coming back to his heated, successful senatorial battle against Helen Gahagan Douglas, a liberal Democratic opponent whom Nixon had accused (perhaps rightly) of being soft on communism. In the Senate he had taken the lead in supporting Whittaker Chambers and in interrogating Alger Hiss, whom Chambers had accused of being a Communist agent—and who had perjured himself. Since Nixon had been known as a bulwark of anticommunism, the anti-anticommunists of the fourth estate had never forgiven his "red-baiting," and each time he worked at placating his great adversary he was denied credit for acts that would have won the goodwill of the media if they had come from a certified figure of the left.

It was Nixon who started the ball rolling for affirmative action for minorities in 1969 with the Philadelphia Plan, an executive directive that provided blacks with preferential access to government contracts. During his presidency, moreover, the size and reach of the American welfare state grew more than it would under any of his presidential successors. Nixon also tried to moderate the U.S.'s prosecution of the Cold War, an act that did please the media but did not really alter his image in the press. Nixon opened the door to relations with Maoist China, a monstrous tyranny led by a mass murderer but one dearly beloved by the *New York Times* and the *Washington Post*. Even in 1999, a work published long after his political career had ended, Nixon continued to make propitiatory offerings to the evil spirits that relentlessly pursued him. He stressed "the need to rectify the inequalities from which blacks and other minorities suffer," and he made unmistakable reference to the "blot on our past" that had resulted from the deferment of the realization of racial equality.

Nixon possibly believed such statements, and I have often encountered characterizations of him as a particularly ill-tempered representative of the Eastern liberal wing of the Republican Party. But there are two problems with this characterization. One, given that American politics have veered sharply to the left since the 1960s on a wide range of social issues, it is unclear that such terms as "Eisenhower Republican" and "Kennedy Democrat" make much sense any more. Conceivably someone might follow FDR or Kennedy in favoring the power of organized labor while rejecting such relatively newfangled notions as gay marriage, feminism, or the required celebration of Martin Luther King as a national icon. Although Pat Buchanan has acquired the reputation of being a right-wing extremist, one could easily imagine him as a prolabor, socially traditional Catholic Democrat of the 1950s. Most ideological labels become dated by the time they are used.

It also strains credulity that the media were really shocked that on certain tapes Nixon uttered a few expletives or that the political enemies he mentioned were disproportionately Jewish. The fact that he surrounded himself with Jewish advisors from the outset of his career makes his suspected anti-Semitism even more open to question. In comparison to Harry Truman, Woodrow Wilson, and Abraham Lincoln, all steady heroes of the left, our thirty-seventh president was a model of political correctness. If the liberal establishment wishes to apply the current standard of sensitive discourse, it should judge those in the past who failed to measure up to its test consistently—or else suspend that presentist standard. I would be delighted if popular historians opted for the second course. But failing that, I would urge the application of a Fairness Doctrine. If intellectuals bestow on the (at least in his conversation) racially insensitive Truman or the obsessively racist Wilson a special indulgence, then fairness requires extending the same courtesy to Nixon. By current standards of sensitivity, as opposed to some crassly selective standard of measurement, Nixon does not stand out as a notably prejudiced president.

Second, and more importantly, there is much in Nixon's writing and persona that does not fit the preconceived image of a "liberal Republican." I suspect that his numerous enemies on the left have noticed this, which may be one of the reasons, as I pointed out in *National Review*, that they despised "Tricky Dick." The attempt by some authors to present his foreign-policy statements as evidence that he stood to the left of Ronald Reagan and Reagan's neoconservative advisors is plainly wrong. Nixon belonged to a tradition of pessimistic realism that would place him well to the right of his neo-Wilsonian critics—that is, to those who assailed the policy of détente with the Soviets that he pursued with Henry Kissinger in the early '70s. The question is not whether this approach was correct. It is rather whether it was actuated by conservative assumptions about politics and human nature. By this criterion Nixon was more conservative than the global democratic crusaders, whom the anticommunist wing of his party happily embraced and often misunderstood.

For me, Nixon's references to "power" in our conversations, in his writing on the Gorbachev era for *Foreign Affairs* (an essay that he shared with me in 1990 before it came out), and in his relevant public statements may be the key to understanding his worldview. He was thoroughly Hobbesian, in the sense that, like the great English materialist philosopher of the seventeenth century, Nixon thought that violence was inherent in human nature. The purpose of statecraft was to institutionalize and restrict the manifestations of an all-too-human propensity. Moreover, Nixon believed, this goal had to be achieved in an age that was obsessed with ideologies. Like other conservative realists, such as George Kennan and James Kurth, he was afraid that appealing to utopian visions, a virtual precondition for taking power in a democratic age, worked against moderation in the conduct of international affairs. On the other hand, he also believed that "Hobbes would have understood the need for oratory," as he once told me. In a letter of January 2, 1991, he admitted apropos of a "fascinating" critique of Woodrow Wilson that I had published and sent to him that despite his disagreement with "a number of Wilson's policies, I think that you will agree that he had a unique ability to convey a sense of mission and idealism." Somewhat strangely he was drawn to Wilson, a paradigmatic democratic crusader whom he never resembled.

Nixon believed that statesmen must appeal to idealism in a modern democratic society: therefore, he admired what he viewed as the "unique ability" to stir public idealism even among those whose statecraft he considered defective. This may have been the tragedy of his public life, his attempt to play a role as an orator and visionary that he necessarily bungled because of his personality and disinclination for idealism. Like John Adams and John Quincy Adams, Nixon was a brooding political thinker who fitted badly into a job that depended on public favor. He wanted the necessary power to shape foreign policy, but he disliked the means by which he had to arrive at a position of authority. He also tended in his memoirs and in conversation to speak about "matters of historical importance," but for him history and its models came for the most part out of a predemocratic age. This was fully apparent from a letter he scribbled to me on April 15, 1992, after having read my review of his latest book, *Seize the Moment*. Responding to my observation that the author was still looking for ways to square rational statecraft with Wilsonian idealism, Nixon explained: "While in order to get Americans to support a strong foreign policy, it is necessary to appeal to their idealism, we must base our creations on hard headed realism. Practical idealism seems to be a contradiction in terms but if the leader has no illusions about what is possible, it is the only approach which will work in this country."

An equally revealing letter, written on March 23, 1990, in response to an essay of mine on the governing principles of Benjamin Disraeli, dwelled on the real reasons for his professed admiration for my subject: "Contrary to the public impression, I was never under the illusion that Disraeli was a closet liberal. He was, in fact, a brilliant practical politician whose heart was not with the working class voters he enfranchised, but with the land-owning Tories whose approval he craved." Never would I have imagined that my correspondent, any more than the nineteenth-century prime minister who invented "Tory democracy," had his "heart" with the common man, save as a means toward a particular end. Indeed, I could not imagine that Nixon would have admired Disraeli as a "brilliant practical politician" if either he or Disraeli had been a true egalitarian.

One of Nixon's favorite terms was "skull session," and it referred to the context in which he believed that political and international problems had to be settled, far from the madding crowd. One of his many books, which he painstakingly fleshed out in longhand on a yellow legal pad, was *Leaders* (1982), a work that reflected his preferred approach to "matters of historical importance." In this book, Nixon recalled his personal meetings with and impressions of world leaders. The operative assumption is that even those who, like the Chinese Communist Chou En-lai, did not support the American side in the Cold War had to be treated as figures of substance who functioned on a historical stage. In an expression of historical realism that might have brought a sense of horror to some anticommunists, Nixon once explained to me: "In the U.S. I don't want Communist traitors around, but in China they are the establishment."

I intuitively understood what he meant, and in a later book on the postcommunist Left I expressed the same sentiment: while ruling Communists in some non-Western countries behaved brutally at times, their intellectual cheering gallery in Western countries was a thousand times more dangerous than they.

At a dinner that Nixon arranged for me and several guests at his home in Saddle River, New Jersey, in October 1992, he also used the term "skull session" to describe the evening's activities. Those who were present—they included Claes Ryn, *Chronicles* editor Thomas Fleming, Forrest McDonald, and CUNY graduate professor George Schwab—were treated to a long, brilliant disquisition on world affairs from a distinguished elder statesman. At another dinner to which I had been invited three years earlier, Nixon had spoken with comparable insight about the same general subject. What struck me on both occasions was how deeply Nixon continued to think about international relations after his retirement from public life. Equally remarkable was the absence of rancor or ideological passion in what he had to say.

The relevant biographies, whether the substantive, three-volume work by Stephen E. Ambrose or the wordy hatchet jobs of Garry Wills and other detractors, all ignore one endearing quality of Nixon's: his sense of humor. His anecdotes about his political career and about those whom he had met in the course of it were sometimes hilarious. The most enjoyable story, partly because it was one that Nixon relished telling, concerned an awkward encounter in the men's room of a D.C. hotel during Nixon's short time in the Senate. As he entered, he noticed that Senator Joe McCarthy had put a headlock on gossip columnist and liberal gadfly Drew Pearson. Both combatants were sweating profusely, and the junior senator from Wisconsin was screaming at Pearson for having written "lots of lies" about him. Nixon proceeded to separate his two acquaintances, while underlining his special qualification as a mediator: "Like Drew, I am a Quaker, but like Joe, I am a Republican senator." Nixon then offered this less than sympathetic observation: "Pearson ran away like a rat that had been cornered but was able to escape." He furrowed his forehead and continued: "I obviously made a mistake. The next day that SOB published dirt about me. I should have let Joe knock the hell out of him." Indeed, although Nixon rarely recounted his setbacks, he became emotional whenever he mentioned Pearson, a long-dead critic, who had failed to repay his good turn after he had rescued him from "Joe's fury."

An even funnier memory of my encounters with Nixon, although it did not seem so at the time, relates to my arrival at his apartment in Saddle River for a dinner in October 1992. Although I had been sent reminders about the exact dinner time and had even collaborated in constructing the guest list, traffic on the Jersey Turnpike delayed my arrival by about thirty-five minutes. To this day I believe that one of the guests I had recommended had revealed my shameful secret: that I am a notorious latecomer for anything to which I am invited. When I rushed into the living room where the other guests had already assembled, my host exuded good will. He insisted on mixing for me his favorite cocktail, which contained lots of gin, which he said he had prepared for world dignitaries, and which he was sure I would appreciate. I swallowed about half the drink with one great gulp. Thereupon the room began to whirl. Until the time we were called to dinner about twenty minutes later, I could barely rise from my chair. In fact, I spent the rest of the night trying to collect my wits; and if I seemed unusually reticent at dinner, it was because my mind was barely working. Not until hours later, when I left for home, did I feel sufficiently confident to handle my car. The next day I awoke with a slight hangover—but a strong memory of having been served one helluva drink.

The question to which I have periodically returned was whether this drink had any effect on Nixon's negotiations with other statesmen. Perhaps it had the effect of breaking down their resistance to his proposals; or perhaps these "leaders" had better alcohol tolerance than I. Another possibility is that the former president had punished me for my late arrival. He had sent me a pointed warning not to come late again and had conveyed his message in a way that could not be interpreted as an act of malice.

After this blurred dinner our paths crossed less frequently, albeit not for reasons attached to that stupefying drink. Both of us faced the same draining problem of wives who were terminally ill: Pat Nixon was then suffering from lung cancer, perhaps contracted from years of heavy smoking; my own spouse, Dana, was dealing with breast cancer, from which she passed away on February 25, 1994, three months, minus two days, before Richard Nixon himself. That may have been the most anguished period of my life. During that time I lost a number of family members in addition to my wife of twenty-five years, and it was hard to maintain contacts with acquaintances beyond my own five children, who were then coping with their mother's fatal illness and eventual death. I did watch snatches of the Nixon funeral and despite my other, more pressing concerns in April 1994, the ceremony moved me profoundly. More than the speeches by the assembled dignitaries, it was the saddened faces of his still handsome and dignified daughters and sons-in-law that stirred me most. Despite his professional imbroglios, the former president's family somehow remained outside "the arena," the term by which Nixon designated the world of partisan strife in which so much of his life had been spent.

At Nixon's home, a lovely young lady then studying at Columbia, Monica Crowley, and a writing assistant, John Taylor, were usually on hand. Both corresponded with me, and Monica was particularly kind in indicating how much she had learned from my books and articles. Fortunately for her future career as a Fox News commentator, Monica seems to have been unaffected by anything I sent her boss. Nor do I think that John, a future director of the Nixon Library at Yorba Linda, followed my perilous lead by assailing Wilsonian idealism. As I joked with Claes Ryn years later, it was the assistants and not the guests at the Nixon home who knew how to play the media game.

A similar observation came to mind when I saw one of my eldest daughter's Rockford high-school classmates, Heather Nauert, as a Chicago commentator on Fox. Heather's mother, whom I recall as an attractive socialite, had leaned toward liberal Republican John B. Anderson against Ronald Reagan in the Illinois primary in 1980. I myself had been a Reagan alternate delegate and had spent the evening of the 1980 primary with Nancy Reagan in the arboretum at Rockford's Sinissippi Park. But it was clearly Heather and her mother who had prospered in the party; and they did so by being more sensitive than I was (or cared to be) to whither the political wind was blowing. These neighbors were ahead of the curve when they took the socially liberal positions in 1980 that the Republican Party may now be moving toward in its efforts to reach leftward. My late father-in-law was fond of observing that the true iron law of social development was less the inevitability of elites than the success of careerists. Elites could not establish themselves without those who advanced themselves by being followers.

A final memory concerning my relationships with Richard Nixon and Pat Buchanan goes back to my presence at the dedication of the former president's library, which abuts his boyhood home in Yorba Linda. Although I received notice about the dedication ceremony and the subsequent dinner in Los Angeles scheduled for July 19, 1990, I acted true to form by forgetting to buy tickets for the events. The president of Elizabethtown College, where I was then working, offered to defray the cost of my fare to Los Angeles and of my stay there if I could establish a "useful contact" with Nixon's long-time supporter Walter Annenberg. It seems that Annenberg, who became one of the wealthiest men in Philadelphia, had studied at the Peddie School in Highstown, New Jersey, with a later biology professor at Elizabethtown, Phares Hertzog, who had recently died in the company of his pet snakes at the age of 107. Annenberg apparently revered the memory of this eccentric bachelor, who from all accounts had been a Pennsylvania Dutch original and who had justifiably claimed to be the "oldest living Boy Scout."

I did obtain my dinner ticket after having spoken to Pat, who had arrived before me. Pat not only managed to get hold of one of the few tickets that was still available but also made sure that I sat near the head table. There, beside Richard Nixon and his family, Bob Hope, the Reverend Norman Vincent Peale, and other easily recognized celebrities of the 1950s, sat Annenberg, who had been

Nixon's ambassador to the Court of Saint James and between 1942 and 1969 owner of the *Philadelphia Inquirer*. His family illustrated a true rags-to-riches story, beginning with his father Moses, an Eastern European Jewish immigrant who had made a fortune publishing papers for horse-racing fans and professional gamblers. There was much that I was eager to ask Annenberg, particularly about the leftward lunge of his once conservative newspaper after its sale to Knight Newspapers twenty years earlier. Alas, by the time I got to meet him all that he wished to discuss, as soon as I mentioned that magical name, was Phares Hertzog. He oozed with affection for this hermit, who had once tied him up in his bed to keep him from escaping academic captivity and who had spent many years of his life living, by choice, in a trailer. Despite the zaniness of his mentor, Annenberg seemed to enjoy my company for no other reason than the fact of my identification with an institution to which Phares had gone after leaving the Peddie School. Not surprisingly, a few weeks after the dinner Annenberg gave Elizabethtown a million dollars for a new building that still bears his famous name.

There was one encounter that I failed to make at the Century Plaza Hotel, the site of the dinner, in the period between the ceremony at Yorba Linda and the evening festivities. While standing in the lobby, waiting for Pat and his wife Shelley, I noticed that I was standing about ten feet away from Henry Kissinger. He was considerably more wrinkled and grey than he had been during his tenure as secretary of state. I somehow had thought that he would look more youthful. My first impulse was to greet Kissinger and mention our shared backgrounds. Both of us came from Central European families that had escaped from the Nazi regime, and we both spoke fluent German, although Kissinger had been born in Europe and retained a distinctive accent. I had read with admiration *A World Restored*

(1957), his study of the Congress of Vienna and his defense of its conservative realism. My first published contribution to *National Review* in 1972 had been a glowing tribute to Kissinger's scholarship and his antirevolutionary Austro-German model of statecraft, Prince Metternich.

But then I had second thoughts that kept me from introducing myself. Perhaps Kissinger was anxiously awaiting an associate or friend. I had no desire to disturb his undoubtedly busy schedule; besides, he might find my conversation, in English or *auf deutsch*, insufferably dull. I was also waiting for the Buchanans, who might suddenly arrive and strike up a conversation that Kissinger wanted no part of. How was I to know? I decided not to start an exchange that might have turned out badly.

As things developed, I only succeeded in speaking to Pat for a few fleeting moments in the hotel lobby, as he was rushing to keep an appointment. Immediately afterwards I regretted my decision not to introduce myself to Kissinger because of a sudden, uncharacteristic hesitation.

I did get to enjoy a consolation prize on the return flight to D.C. This was the opportunity to converse with another former secretary of state, Al Haig, who sat beside me on the plane. Haig was meticulously dressed in a dark business suit, carried an attaché case brimful of folders, and had obviously recently acquired hearing aids for both ears. Despite the verbal awkwardness and malapropisms that I associated with his public appearances, he managed to speak well on a number of subjects. He knew and admired both Kissinger and Nixon, having served as Kissinger's assistant during the Nixon presidency. He claimed to respect their "realistic understanding of the world," a desirable quality that he wished me to believe he had tried to emulate as Reagan's secretary of state. Haig avoided those phrases I had found especially tiresome when he had used them in office. Gone were his pompous, neo-Churchillian references to "the democracies" and his dubious observations about "how democracies have never fought each other." On the long flight back to Washington, I found something congenial about this man whose phraseology in the past had often made me cringe with discomfort. I thought about his colorful beginnings as an Irish Catholic Republican in Irish Democratic Philadelphia—and of the long row he had had to hoe in order to reach his recent eminence. By the time we parted at the Washington National Airport, I had actually come to like Al Haig. What I cannot say is that my conversation with him made up for my failure to speak to the figure I had hesitated to approach at the Century Plaza Hotel on the preceding evening. That is a chance which will not likely return.

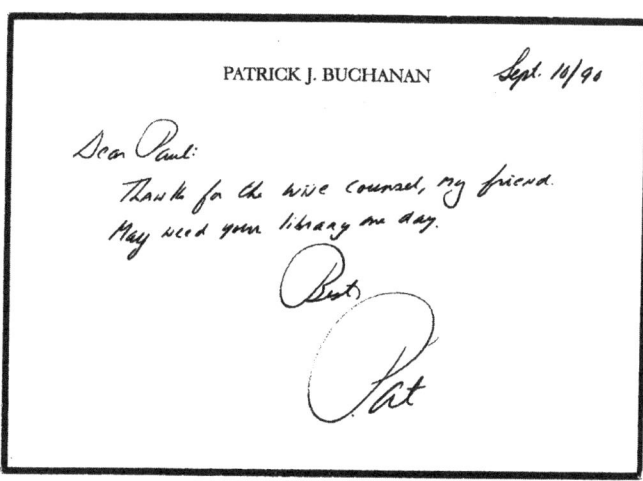

RICHARD NIXON

June 30, 1989

577 CHESTNUT RIDGE ROAD
WOODCLIFF LAKE, NEW JERSEY

Dear Paul,

    This is just a note to tell you how much I appreciated your piece in <u>National Review</u>.

    You will undoubtedly get some heat for it from both the right and the left, but I want you to know that at least one of NR's readers liked the very generous appraisal from a recognized intellectual!

    With warm regards,

Sincerely,

Dr. Paul Gottfried

VIII

Reconciliations

The connections discussed in this chapter among three now deceased friends are neither contrived nor forced. Whatever their differences might have been, certain characteristics linked Russell Kirk (1918–94), Sam Francis (1923–94), and Murray Rothbard (1926–95). I remember the three of them talking together at a 1993 meeting that Pat Buchanan had called in a Virginia hotel just outside of Washington. The meeting had been organized to come up with advisors for a new foundation, The American Cause (an enterprise whose name had been taken from a book of that title published by Russell in 1957). The foundation would serve as the intellectual nucleus for a second presidential campaign (the first having taken place the year before) that Buchanan would launch in the near future. Although the attendees got on well, for the most part, sharp disagreement eventually surfaced between Sam and Russell. Given Russell's usual reserve, it was not surprising that his wife Annette defended her husband's views in the ensuing battle of ideas. The two discussants could not agree on whether the cause that needed defending was to be "conservative" or "right wing."

I tried to stay out of the fray, but my facial expressions might have indicated to Annette that I was taking Sam's side, even though

Russell's spouse was correct on the broad questions at issue. I was being outwardly deferential to her husband, who had been especially hospitable to me when, as a young professor at Michigan State many years before, I had first visited him and Annette at their home in Mecosta. In any case, Sam was needling an older man who already suffered from a heart ailment. And his target was not some run-of-the-mill, cable-television intellectual but someone who had helped to lay the theoretical foundations for postwar American conservatism—and whose sweet, serene disposition was proverbial. When Sam explained, "I am not a conservative but a man of the Right, perhaps of the far Right," one suspected that sparks would soon fly. Sam had recently brought out an anthology of essays, *Beautiful Losers* (1994), in which he attacked those "archaic conservatives" whom he saw as posturing and clinging to cultural artifacts. Sam had condemned Russell, at least indirectly, for not having adapted his rhetoric and image to the times.

Sam's argument about changing ideologies and the historical and social dimensions of political movements carried for me considerable weight. This friend had devoted his writing and speaking career to saying things that I thought needed to be said: e.g., that the bourgeois age in Western modernity was already passing; that our political and to some extent social life was dominated by a managerial class pushing an egalitarian ideology; and that the only way in which the Right, however one defined it, could offer effective opposition to managerial tyranny was through a mass movement. That movement was to be based, Sam argued (following the French social thinker Georges Sorel), on the propagation of a "redemptive myth."

Sam never made entirely clear how this invented "myth" would work to achieve his end. The primitive Christian church, in which Sorel had located the power of a successful myth, truly believed its message about the end of days. Early Christians went to their deaths bearing witness to God's promise of redemption. But such would not be true for the kind of mass leader whom Sam had in mind. Such a figure would be intrinsically different from those fearless leaders of the early church and of the anarchist movement (both of which Sorel cited to illustrate his thesis). What was now supposedly needed was a social redeemer who would devise an end-of-days scenario for political purposes. With some luck, Sam's temporal savior would turn the average yuppie family into a raging opponent of the Equal Employment Opportunity Commission.

Sam's view of social history was not without cogency—particularly his insistence that broad political movements need social contexts in order to prevail. American "conservatism," he explained, no longer exists in any political and experiential sense that would be recognizable to someone from the early nineteenth century. Sam rightly contended that the bourgeois, predominantly small-town American society that had fashioned the interwar Right had lost most of its social and cultural force. What Main Street, mostly Protestant Americans had understood as their "political tradition" was becoming for most contemporary Americans, including Republicans, a vague memory from the distant past. That the neoconservatives and their subordinates became the mainstream "conservative movement" in the '80s did not surprise Sam. If the revised American "tradition" had become a project of cooperation between welfare-state managers, multinational corporate interests, and the media industry, this intertwining of managerial elites could and would not produce anything that could be reasonably considered to be "conservative." Constituting a status quo is not the same as standing for a social order. Today's conservatism, Sam never tired of pointing out, means keeping those in power from losing out to those who might challenge them.

Such bracing ideas, which found their way into a recently published book of mine on changing "conservative values," met with a mixed response from Sam's auditors. By then, however, I was wondering what positive good Pat and his sister Bay thought would come of this gathering. What they needed was advice from someone who would be able to get Pat lots of votes on Election Day. While the present company was more honorable and more interesting than this hypothetical strategist, my friends did not strike me as being well suited to manipulating the public. Sam and Murray Rothbard went on about how Pat would do better at the polls if he ran a second time. The "people," they explained, were eager to break loose. Sam might have said such things with less than sincere conviction, in order to incite a populist revolt. His position that day was that while the masses are still basically decent, the elites are the ones who needed fixing. He assured us that it was only a matter of time before the differences between the "two classes" would erupt into an open break. That would lead to a "Middle American revolt" which would surge out of the "heartland." Whether this heartland referred to a place of the heart, a geographic region, or a sociological category was never fully explained.

While Sam might have been speaking in a calculating way, Murray rallied to the same position with real zeal. The author of dozens of erudite texts on economics and economic history, a spirited libertarian polemicist, and one of the greatest living exponents of Austrian economics, Murray, who was by then in his mid-sixties, still looked forward to the moment when "the people would awake." Unlike most of the other graying dignitaries in the room that evening, Murray was the genuine populist article. Russell and I certainly were not. Though we may have differed over whether "conservatism" was a socially possible political option, Russell and I did not differ in our estimation of the "people." When I was recently invited to discuss with libertarians from the Cato Institute whether the people have the government they deserve, I responded to the effect that "the government is far better than the one that the masses actually merit." I doubt that Russell would have come to a different conclusion.

An unfathomable mystery from my perspective is how rightwing populists who often stress the doctrine of original sin forget their grim theology when they turn to politics. If one truly believes that human nature is fallen, save for the intervention of divine grace, why do sinners suddenly become angelic when they make electoral decisions? And if populists are discontent with how their fellow citizens vote for those who support government favors at the expense of other taxpayers, for increasingly unprotected borders, and for giving away power to social engineers and state-sponsored sensitivity trainers, why do they inconsistently absolve the "people" of all responsibility for their role in this outcome? Why do they make it appear as if the "people" have nothing to do with endorsing the servile state under which they live? It is allegedly not the "people" who have done this to themselves. They are simply the innocent dupes of the political class. Like Russell, who preached "authority" and "degrees and hierarchy," I grimaced when the others talked positively about the "people."

It has never seemed to me a convincing argument that the public is being deceived when voters pick from among those limited options the elites place before them. As public-opinion polls suggest, most Americans are pleased with their governing system. Tens of millions of Americans swear undying allegiance to our two national parties. And whatever success the supposedly more constitutionally restrained Republicans have had in winning elections often can be attributed to their willingness to imitate their more openly "big-government" opposition. Democrats accomplish their ends with less double talk by expanding government and managerial control while transferring income as patronage. Hamilton's view of the "people" as a "beast" is only partly accurate. More to the point is Plato's understanding that most people never subdue their appetites and passions in order to rule over themselves, let alone others, by applying "*logistikon* [reasoning power]." But since public administration and the media now direct our lives and opinions, Plato's teaching about self-control may have become politically irrelevant. No longer is there any need for prudential reason as a check on the intemperate elements of our nature. People have outsourced this task through their certified votes to social professionals.

All three of the figures remembered in this chapter entertained their own visions about where the country should be moving. But at least two of them offered the unlikely scenario that the "people" would vote, against all predictions, for Pat. Since Russell and I felt in our bones that this would never happen, the American future as envisaged by our companions seemed to us an exercise in wishful thinking. For Murray, however, Pat's run for the presidency would bring about a return to the world of gun-bearing, self-accountable citizens whom he had celebrated in *Conceived in Liberty* (four volumes, 1975–79) and in his other studies of an older, less bureaucratically captive America. Murray's idealism was on display when he addressed the Old Right organization the John Randolph Club on January 18, 1992, during Buchanan's first campaign for the Republican nomination. To the satisfaction of the *National Review* observers, who were plainly looking for evidence of right-wing immoderateness, and to the jubilant applause of his disciples, Murray ended his stemwinder with this peroration: "With the inspiration of the death of the Soviet Union before us, we know that it can be done. With Pat Buchanan as our leader, we shall break the clock of social democracy.

We shall break the clock of the Great Society. We shall break the clock of the welfare state. We shall break the clock of the New Deal. We shall break the clock of Woodrow Wilson's New Freedoms and perpetual war. We shall repeal the twentieth century."

Needless to say, Pat did not win, and even if he had, it is unlikely that he would have done what the neoconservatives and liberals feared: abolish the managerial state from which flowed their jobs and sustenance. Buttressing Murray's optimism, however, was a confidence that history could be turned back, and that this would happen because the "people," once the scales had been lifted from their eyes, would choose "liberty" over big government. Behind this vision stood the shadows of such late-eighteenth- and early-nineteenth-century democrats as Tom Paine and James Mill, men who had believed that mass suffrage would end government's control over the lives of tax-burdened subjects. According to such thinkers, it was restricted voting rights and the exclusion of the "people" from power that caused the state to expand and grow arrogant. That a "democratic welfare state" would behave in an even more predatory fashion was unimaginable to these advocates of universal (manhood) suffrage.

Russell, by contrast, dreamed not of the people liberated from bureaucratic shackles but of the more limited benefits that might result from a Buchanan victory. Being back home in the pine barrens of central Michigan, with the knowledge of having achieved some political good, and being able to enjoy the confidence and respect of a friendly government might have been all that he wished for. A paterfamilias already advanced in years, Russell was hoping to provide for his four daughters and his wife. But this did not entail for him the acquisition of insurance and pension plans, newfangled notions that he tried to avoid. (Russell was deeply suspicious of insurance and of all who trafficked in this dubious item.)

He and his wife had chaired Buchanan's 1992 primary campaign in Michigan, but this venture into partisan politics might have brought more political excitement than Russell had wanted. During Reagan's presidency, he had been offered a director's position or some other unspecified patronage plum in Washington. Russell had turned down the offer as soon as he learned that the job would require him to leave Michigan and appear every day in an office. (Writing and napping in his small library down the block from his house was the closest Russell ever came, or wanted to come, to a nine-to-five job.) Although Russell had published strings of books and articles, and although his works *The Conservative Mind* (1953) and *Eliot and His Age* (1971) had been featured in the national press, it is doubtful that he ever set his sights on an academic post befitting his achievements. The most he had hoped to receive from the Reagan administration, which he had initially welcomed, was the opportunity to present the Jefferson Lecture in the Humanities, an honor that brings a sizeable honorarium and is sponsored by the National Endowment for the Humanities. Even this honor was not to be his, inasmuch as the neoconservatives, who then dominated the NEH board, had no use for him or his work. (This I learned from our mutual friend Peter Stanlis, who sat on that board.) By 1992, Russell's personal ambitions, and his belief in the possibility of a "conservative" transformation of the country, belonged to his and the country's past.

In all likelihood Sam had no greater hopes of personal success, despite his ritual invocations of the "people." In the 1970s and 1980s he had talked about "Middle American Radicals," then leaning on the research of Michigan scholar Donald Warren, who had examined the combination of reactionary and radical attitudes among economically and socially desperate Americans. The types of people Warren and Sam had investigated were the ones the populists had hoped to recruit and who naturally spooked journalists and academicians. They also constituted a declining percentage of the work force in a postindustrial economy and had nothing in common with those the media and public educators had already socialized. Sam recognized that he was betting on a fading horse. He also glumly observed that further Hispanic immigration would lead to a society in which his views had no place at all. As the '90s progressed, his glumness grew more perceptible, particularly after he was ousted from the staff of the *Washington Times* for his accumulated indiscretions. The fact that he had previously won national prizes at the *Times* as an editorial writer and that his stunning analytic intelligence vastly exceeded that of his detractors rendered his fall even more painful for him and his numerous admirers.

The straw that broke the camel's back was a speech Sam delivered at a 1994 conference held by *American Renaissance*, a publication that has been properly described as "soft racialist." Had the speech been given in a different setting, it might not have unleashed the same intense reactions. And in all likelihood, Sam's remarks about the ethnic basis of Western culture would not have rattled earlier mainstream American audiences. Forty years earlier such commentary might have been seen as furnishing food for thought. (His offending words, by the way, figure prominently in Buchanan's best-selling book *State of Emergency*. Pat might have put them there out of agreement with, as well as obvious respect for, their author.)

If a similar oration had been given by a black or Hispanic nationalist about his cultural identity, Sam observed, it might have been favorably mentioned in the *New York Times* or the *Washington Post*. Several years later, Sam showed me excerpts from a speech that had been given by Douglas Feith, a neoconservative policy advisor to George W. Bush. It was a speech that Michael Lind had critically discussed in the *Nation*. Sam correctly noted that Feith demanded a degree of Jewish ethnic solidarity that his allies in the U.S. would have denounced as neo-Nazi if Anglo-Saxon Protestants had asked for the same group recognition. Feith denied to Christians the right to the kind of collective allegiance that he demanded for his coethnics.

While Sam correctly perceived the implicit double standard, he could not bring himself to admit that those whom it harmed were willing to live with the slight. If my friend hoped to survive as a journalist in the present society, he would have to stay away from "insensitive" subjects. The alternative, it seemed to me, was to do something that did not require direct contact with the media, the priests of the PC religion. In the world of communications, doctrinal conformity would likely remain the established rule.

The last years of Sam's abbreviated life (he died, at age fifty-seven, of the effects of an aneurysm in February 2005) were spent amid his myriad books on the third floor of Robert E. Lee's childhood home on Cameron Street in Alexandria, Virginia. The ample working space and a salary that allowed Sam to continue turning out his syndicated column were the gifts of a marvelous patroness, Sylvia Crutchfield. Sylvia, who had perceived in her otherwise professionally abandoned beneficiary the marks of genius, went about the country raising money on his behalf. Although I often disagreed with his conclusions and found his hortatory prose to be sometimes forgettable, at his best—a level that he often reached, particularly in his columns for *Chronicles* magazine—Sam was a brilliant stylist and courageous analyst. Although my junior by five years, he was the contemporary on the American Right who shaped my thinking most decisively. As a frequent dinner guest at our home in Bethesda, Maryland, during my years of service at *The World and I*, and as someone who produced many provocative texts, Sam occupies a special place among my mentors. Whatever my personal setbacks, I resent what happened to him more than I do my own tribulations. While I have managed to survive my enemies, this was not true for my reclusive friend, who expressed unseasonable thoughts all too loudly. According to both of my wives, I was a better friend to Sam than he was to me or to most anyone else whose company he frequented. This was especially true of his friendship with a gracious woman, Franny Griffin, whom Sam dated for decades but (alas) never married. (His inflexible bachelor habits became more obstinate with age.) But that is in the nature of friendship, which does not have to be a relation between those who are equally attached to each other. In an imperfect world, most friendships I have witnessed do not live up to Aristotle's ideal.

Despite his often impenetrable solitude and gruff exterior, Sam was much closer in his personal qualities to Murray and Russell than he might have been willing to recognize. Not one of these figures possessed the burning careerist ambition of Beltway "conservative" journalists. If offered the salaries of Fox news commentators and *Weekly Standard* celebrities, my friends would not have known how to spend such largess. Like Will Herberg, they thirsted for what they understood as righteousness. They exemplified Socrates' prayer that one should "be content with those riches that lie within." Sam was as much a "beautiful loser" as those he mocked, and this was to his credit as well as theirs. What made these figures "beautiful losers" was their willingness to forego worldly success for what they believed. At Sam's graveside service in his hometown of Chattanooga, at which I stood among the mourners, the officiating minister told us about how he had just read the work of this onetime member of his congregation who had moved to Washington. The pious minister commented on the otherworldly devotion to truth and honesty that he encountered in Sam's work.

A similar tribute would apply to Murray Rothbard, whom I came to know in the late '80s, after having met him at a conference hosted by the Rockford Institute. Despite his admiration for those who had accumulated wealth and for the vainglorious New York Yankees (I have been a Dodgers fan since the 1950s), Murray never revealed an acquisitive side, save for his penchant for dusty books. His New York apartment, which I once visited, looked as if he and his wife Joey had used every inch of their property as a depository for manuscripts and journals. Although I never saw their dwelling in Las Vegas, where Murray went to accept a professorship in economics at the University of Nevada, I cannot imagine that it was any less cluttered than his apartment three thousand miles away.

From the time I first met Murray, in what was intended to be the fleshing out of an alliance between paleocons and paleolibertarians (a goal that was never quite achieved), he tested my independent judgment. Although I failed in my response to the baseball-preference test, I did well by smiling sympathetically when Murray opined that Kaiser Bill had been a "really good guy." Not that I thought that the German Kaiser was any less scatterbrained than he actually was, but I agreed with the sentiments behind the compliment. Like Murray, I thought that the Allied side in 1914 and afterwards had behaved as irresponsibly as their German-Austrian adversaries. I also agreed with Murray's judgment that the U.S. should not have been drawn into the savage European conflict as a belligerent but could have served more honestly as a peace broker. But I did express surprise when I was told that Herbert Hoover as president had conducted himself in the "same statist, spendthrift fashion as FDR." It was only after I had purchased Murray's revisionist study *America's Great Depression* (1963) that it became clear to me that FDR's predecessor had pursued some of the same policies later associated with the New Deal.

Murray's take on American economic and administrative history went against the mainstream historiography that had been inflicted on me in college. Although the progressivist interpretation, one stressing great executive transformations punctuated by just wars, had offended my sense of measure, it was Murray who confirmed what I had merely intuited. The hagiography of Arthur Schlesinger and others of his ilk seemed extravagant in both its praise and deprecations. It awakened doubts even in a focused Europeanist like me, who had only dabbled in Americana. Murray took his sources without regard to creed, even from such blatantly leftist historians as Gabriel Kolko and William Appleman Williams. With piles of statistics, he built his arguments showing the quantum leaps and corresponding corruptness of an American corporate state, which had continued to expand throughout the twentieth century. (From a younger colleague, David Brown, who has produced a highly readable tome on the Wisconsin school of history, I have learned that Murray's attacks on corporate liberalism might have originated as a "University of Wisconsin idea.")

But what distinguished Murray from his occasional leftist sources was his emphasizing the ascent of the democratic welfare state more than the machinations of bankers and captains of industry. Capitalists, he used to explain, are scoundrels like the rest of humanity; they will therefore take advantage of big government if offered favors. But more relevant is the fact that government can offer such favors; and it can destroy business operations through public administrators. Although Murray detested "government" or "our enemy the state," he had a certain grudging respect for the target of his hate. Never would he have claimed that politics merely reflects "culture" or preexisting values. He properly understood the awesome power that is available to welfare-state administrations, which socialize people and control much of their earnings. Nor did he approach American history as the story of the progress of democratic liberty. Rather, he grasped the loss of what early Americans, whom he deeply respected, had understood as their natural liberties.

Despite my disagreements with Murray, particularly over the social-contract theory of government and his reading of John Locke, I have learned much from his insights on Wilsonianism, democratic administration, and the Great Depression. From his many letters to me, all produced during the last five years of his life, I gained new insight into contemporary American politics. Unlike Russell, who wrote elliptically in his letters about current events, Murray would dwell attentively on such ephemera as a mayoral election in New York or the alleged bickering among the "much beloved neoconservatives." His disciple Lew Rockwell took it upon himself to publish in a single volume Murray's opinion pieces, essays that from 1990 onward came out in the monthly *The Triple R*. Lew's anthology, *The Irrepressible Rothbard* (2000), contains among other gems a set of predictive marvels that chart the later path of the American conservative movement, such as "King Kristol" and "Big Government Libertarians." I can still hear Murray cackling with glee as he typed out these cleverly worded assaults on the American establishment.

Murray also produced a mass of thoughtful movie reviews in which he assaulted pompous films with a joyous abandon. His most entertaining review was a demontage of that tribute to the victims of sexist oppression, *The Piano* (1993), a film set in nineteenth-century Australia and featuring Harvey Keitel and Holly Hunter. Although

The Piano was obviously calling attention to a trendy problem, the abuse inflicted on a deaf woman by her overbearing husband in a frontier situation, Murray insisted that the movie had no detectable dramatic value. It was a political statement whose main attraction was a prolonged view of Holly Hunter's rather ordinary back in an adulterous love scene that dragged on far too long. Murray's withering comments about movies made it impossible for me to continue to enjoy many of the films I had once deemed innocuous.

Murray was an extremely versatile intellectual whose talents never ceased to amaze. A mathematically trained economist who came to challenge econometrics as a science under the influence of his preceptor, the renowned Austrian scholar Ludwig von Mises; a brilliant polemicist on just about any subject; an American economic historian who delighted in taking on statist sacred cows; and a passable writer on neo-Thomist ethics, Murray did everything with flair and prodigious learning. He was finally but not insignificantly "fun to be around," as his wife pointed out, in a way that was true for only a few other people.

That he died suddenly of a massive coronary while accompanying his wife on a visit to an optometrist in New York in January 1995 was upsetting but not entirely unexpected. Murray was notorious for living as he wanted, eating rich foods that he should have stayed away from and ignoring premonitory signs of his cardiac condition. His biographer Justin Raimondo remarked upon the obvious when he mentioned Murray's "general suspicion of doctors."

Even more importantly, Murray burnt himself out as a sparkling personality and conspicuous workaholic. The last year of his life was spent on a history of the great economists, which was intended to demonstrate that early modern Spanish Jesuits, and not Adam Smith and the other figures of the Scottish Enlightenment, engineered the major conceptual breakthroughs leading to free-market economics and, eventually, the Austrian school of economics. In his *An Austrian Perspective on the History of Economic Thought* (1995), Murray again played the maverick, armed with loads of facts and the premise that free-market concepts, such as the use of prices to determine relative market value, were already present in late Scholastic thought. Supposedly, the Austrian school, which took root in a Catholic culture, built on a conceptual universe that Spanish Jesuits had been instrumental in forming.

As a historian, I was deeply skeptical of Murray's genealogical explorations. After all, the alleged breakthroughs of Spanish Jesuits had no impact on the surrounding society, and the Austrian economists were either assimilated Austrian Jews or European liberals (which in Catholic countries usually meant that they were also anticlerical). Moreover, Austrian Thomists, who represented Catholic academic thinking in Austria, scorned Murray's intellectual ancestors, and despite their good relations with the Habsburg dynasty, which hired at least one Austrian economist as a tutor to the crown prince, the free marketeers were strongly discriminated against in Central Europe at clericalist-leaning universities and among politically Catholic faculties. Their ideas were seen there as both alien and as colored by Anglo-Saxon Protestantism.

Less significant than these reservations, however, was my admiration for Murray's bold attempt to prove his argument. Though I myself lean in no small degree toward Max Weber's position on the pivotal role of Calvinist theology and Calvinist cultures in nurturing economic modernity, I nonetheless applauded Murray's pertinacity. In all probability, his multiple trips to various libraries in the New York area, which required trudging back to his apartment with reams of reading matter, contributed to his sudden death. For what purpose,

I later asked, did he jeopardize his life, perhaps only half-admitting to himself the fatal risk he was taking? It was unlikely that his last book, which came from someone who was perceived as being on the fringe, would have brought him praise in New York circles or among academic mandarins. Murray undertook his work as an intellectual exercise or perhaps to demonstrate an intuition that had grown to ripeness in the back of his mind. In any case, his book exacted a price that seems to have been all too costly.

My recollections of Russell Kirk are harder to retrieve than those of Sam Francis and Murray Rothbard. The reason is not that I liked Russell any less or that I valued his achievements less highly. During my early adult years I visited him in Mecosta at least six times. I was among the well-wishers in Chicago in 1984 when Russell received the Ingersoll Prize for his accomplishments. In addition, Russell and I spent time together walking and conversing in Cleveland, Chicago, and Washington. When he delivered a scathing and unexpected indictment of the neoconservatives at the Heritage Foundation in 1988, I sat in the audience with an open mouth, more surprised than delighted by what seemed in this particular context a possibly costly indiscretion. (The speaker was being paid by a then largely neoconservative foundation for his rhetorical services.) I was then working for *The World and I* as the senior editor, and I had come to depend on Russell for his frequent and engrossing contributions to our "Modern Thought Section."

  He nonetheless seems more remote than the other figures in this section because his work and personality affected my life many years earlier. As a student of European conservatism, I had studied his writing while in my mid-twenties. At that time I had acquired an unbounded admiration for Russell's writing aptitude, and I still recall a visit to his home when he banged out in one sleepless night a long, elegantly constructed chapter of his literary prodigy *Eliot and His Age*. Russell personified what the German poet Schiller described as "naïve" as opposed to "sentimental" verbal creativity. His writing was spontaneously brilliant. Everything that he put to paper testified to an unlabored genius. But none of it seemed to come through in Russell's speech, a faculty that he never mastered because of his visible, painful shyness. Having said all this, I should also note that there wasn't much in any technical sense that I could learn from him. Once, while showing him my dissertation in which there are favorable references to his ideas, it crossed my mind that there was nothing he could do to improve my text, save to rewrite it in his own manner.

Russell was a solitary aesthetic marvel who in all likelihood never agonized over his compositions. He would draw a single wreath of smoke out of his cigar each time he paused in his typing—and then he would bring forth what inevitably followed. Watching him type reminded me of an arresting statement that I once heard Leonard Bernstein make about Beethoven. It was Bernstein's contention that even if Beethoven was not the equal of Mozart as a melodist, nobody in the history of music had constructed compositions like his, in which every passage came forth "with ineluctability" from whatever preceded it. No matter how often Beethoven was interrupted in his work, each time he went back to it he devised the only possible combination of notes that could have continued what he had begun before. Russell seemed to write in the same way.

I am exactly the opposite. I must edit awkward drafts before arriving at lucid prose. All of my books have arisen from laboriously detailed outlines, and their transformation into readable texts has grown more and more arduous with age. Besides, I have been heavily influenced by Continental philosophy and, even more ominously, by Franco-German-Italian sociology. Russell had little taste for such Old World exotica, and it was hard to discuss these interests with him during my visits to Mecosta. His wife added to this problem of communication by contrasting my suspicious-sounding Teutonic mentors with her husband's quintessentially Anglo-American traditionalism. She may have had a point.

In any case, by the time I got to know Sam and Murray, Russell and I were bumping into each other less frequently. He fitted into my twenties and was a treasured acquaintance of my late wife Dana, who died a few months before Russell in 1994. It was with Dana and my eldest daughter that I used to visit Russell and Annette in Mecosta, particularly when I was teaching at Case Western Reserve in Cleveland in the late '60s and into the early '70s. With grim determination we would motor along the interstate around Lake Erie and proceed up the Lower Peninsula of Michigan into the pine barrens around Mecosta.

Once, my Volvo station wagon broke down in a hamlet about twenty miles south of our destination, and Russell, who was then sporting long hair, turned up with a groupie and a battered car to rescue us. My wife mistook our rescuers for hippies; she was afraid to ride in their car, since one or both might have been high on drugs. During this same visit, my wife found that she was no longer able to breast-feed my eldest daughter, who was colicky and irritable. Annette, who was nursing, offered to help out, but my daughter would not take another woman's milk. After we had returned home, Russell wrote to explain that his eldest daughter, Monica, had described my wife as "the lady without milk." I wrote back that Monica should have said that "Dana and I were trying to survive with a screaming daughter."

It should be observed that Russell had a dissenting relation to the postwar conservative movement. Although some, for their own purposes, have tried to accentuate his intimate connection to what George Nash calls the "conservative intellectual movement since 1945," and although it would be hard to imagine that movement without his contributions, Russell was a political loner as well as a solitary soul. His biographer, my colleague Wes McDonald, has underscored this fact by noting the political friendships and cultural phobias that more conventional pictures of Kirk fail to mention. Unlike the technocrats of the establishment Right, such as Newt Gingrich, Kirk not only stayed clear of technical innovations but also cultivated a well-known distaste for them. He did his work in a late-nineteenth-century technical setting; he had nothing but contempt for word processors, the operation of which Wes once tried to explain to him. His loathing for television was so extreme that he tried to keep this invention out of the hands of his daughters and house guests. When his young daughters and an Ethiopian refugee who was staying at their home dragged a portable set from a junk pile into their attic and tried to watch it there, Russell lost his temper as soon as he learned of their treachery. He threw the offending object out of the attic window. So much for his openness to American culture, as that phenomenon is understood by millions of his countrymen!

Kirk had been a close friend of the quadrennial Socialist candidate for president Norman Thomas, for whom he voted in 1944; and while they debated some issues that undoubtedly separated them in the public mind, they agreed more often than not on foreign policy, particularly on the desirability of keeping the U.S. out of foreign wars. In this matter Kirk was undoubtedly closer to Thomas than he was to the fervently anti-Soviet *National Review*. My friend Boyd Cathey, a historical archivist in Raleigh, North Carolina, and an intimate of Russell's, recently sent me a collection of Russell's statements published after the Second World War in which he warned his fellow Americans against the temptation of opposing military enemies in a spirit of moral arrogance. Such an attitude, Kirk maintained, had resulted not only in the justified removal of the Nazis from power in Germany but also in the widespread terrorist bombing of a demonized foe and in the persistent attempt to reconstruct the consciousness of what remained of a defeated German nation.

For years Russell wrote for *National Review* on education, but never, as far as I know, on the appropriate limits of America's military policy. In my twenties I happily assumed that he and everyone else at *National Review* agreed on such key issues as the Cold War and the free market; only many years later did I begin to notice the editors' sometimes bitter internal differences. How long it took me to learn the obvious in this case is underscored by the fact that when I met Thomas Fleming in Rockford in the early 1980s, it took Tom several months to convince me of two obvious facts: One, NR's original contributors had disagreed about significant issues; and two, the publication had been generally moving leftward for decades. All that had remained stable were its editors' continuing aversion to communism and their firm allegiance to the GOP. In later life I became preoccupied with these perceptions, which had eluded me for decades.

In the 1970s Russell became thick with Eugene McCarthy, the former antiwar candidate for president, and in 1976 he voted for this onetime figure of the left in the presidential race. By then the two men had discovered their shared interest in poetry and Christian theology and in finding ways to balance economic prosperity with ecological concerns. Eventually the two friends would come to share another position: opposition to what they perceived as a multicultural immigration policy. Kirk did not first discover his differences with the neoconservatives in the mid-1980s, as might be inferred from his controversial speech at the Heritage Foundation about how the neoconservatives had disappointed him. His views had never been in sync with theirs. Tension had lurked, beneath the surface, between his small-town isolationist outlook and the fusion of capitalism and militant anticommunism that came to mark the postwar American Right and its flagship publication, *National Review*.

Russell tended strongly toward a Taft Republican outlook in American politics, and this allowed him in the end to reconsider his relation to someone whom in the past he had objected to as a "sectarian libertarian," Murray Rothbard. Although the Taft Republicanism in Russell's case was not grounded in any cult of the free market, both he and Murray distrusted certain by then permanent features of the American regime: an aggressively internationalist foreign policy and centralized administrative power. While Murray became anathema to the postwar conservative movement for having ridiculed plans to roll back the Iron Curtain, Russell had stayed in that movement to become a founding father. But what Hegel called the "cunning of reason" eventually brought the two together as enemies of America's expanding managerial state and missionary foreign policy. By the 1990s, the two former adversaries fully grasped their common moral ground, something they had failed to comprehend twenty years earlier. But it was a moral ground that only a remnant of their countrymen continued to share. That minority is daily growing even smaller, and it may soon barely exist.

IX

Voices against Progress

As I think back to the 1970s and 1980s, five figures seem to have been particularly important for my thinking during that period. Eugene Genovese (1930–), Christopher Lasch (1932–94), Peter Stanlis (1919–), Robert Nisbet (1913–96), and M. E. "Mel" Bradford (1934–93) came to exert a special influence on me between the time of my arrival at Rockford College in 1973 and my Washington years in the late 1980s. In 1981, Gene, Peter, and I all wrote letters supporting Mel, then a professor of literature at the University of Dallas, when he was under consideration for the chairmanship of the National Endowment for Humanities. After his candidacy foundered following published attacks on him as a pro-Confederate critic of Abraham Lincoln, we continued to defend Mel's reputation in print as both a principled Southern conservative and a genuine literary scholar. Peter, who was then my older colleague at Rockford and who had worked for my appointment at the college, later teamed up with Mel and Gene a second time. Each of them rallied to my aid after I had become a candidate for the NEH chairmanship in 1986.

It was a strange alliance (exemplifying what the Germans call a *Schicksalsgemeinschaft*, an alliance of fate) that united me to Gene, an avowed Marxist at the University of Rochester, and his equally Marxist wife Betsey; to Mel, a Southern agrarian; and to Peter, a Catholic Burkean, all at the same time. But these assorted friends showed no perceptible qualms about cooperating with each other, at least not on my behalf. Indeed, by then Gene had become one of Mel's closest friends. The two stayed in touch through letters and through their membership in the same Southern-based historical societies. Unlike the less generous but more conventional Marxist Eric Foner, who had gone about tarring Mel as a Southern racist, Gene expressed shock that President Reagan would pass over an outstanding Southern traditionalist loyalist in looking for a reliable public servant.

All of my senior advisors wrote letters of advice to me while I was still a live candidate for the chairmanship, that is, before my candidacy dissolved and Lynne Cheney went on to capture the prize. These advisors stressed the need for me to keep a low profile and not to grant compromising interviews if I made it onto the short list. Above all I should not appear to be on the far right—or else I would be taken apart by the staffs of Ted Kennedy and the other liberal Democrats in the Senate. Besides, the neoconservatives, who had helped bring down Mel, would not hesitate to beat my hide just as badly, particularly if they had their own horse in the race. The fact that they had managed to move their point man William Bennett from the NEH up to the post of secretary of education did not mean they had no interest in the lower office, which they had controlled since 1981. Peter was particularly insistent that I should never lose sight of the enemy, having already spent several years on the NEH board fighting skirmishes with the "neocon politicians."

A widely published author on Burke, natural law, and his one-time teacher at Middlebury's Bread Loaf School of English, Robert

Frost, my colleague at Rockford could not forget the war wounds he had sustained in confrontations with other board members. Gene dwelled on the same themes in pungent language and with references to the organizational skill of the Mafia, a group that he held up as a model for the Old Right. He was convinced that I was too soft for my impending battles, although it was hard for me to figure out how making friends on the Hill and lining up recommendations drafted by senatorial staffers was like the bloody imbroglios engaged in by the leaders of organized crime.

It was Gene who wrote for me the longest and most absorbing description of the infighting for the NEH chairmanship, a narrative that concluded with this fateful warning: "For God's sake, keep your mouth shut. Bradford was ruined by being sucked into an interview with the *Washington Post.*" In his unforgettable description he explained the existing alignment of forces in this way:

> The word on the street is that Buckley and the neos are pushing for [Robert] Hollander. I know people who like Hollander and tell me he's a good chap. No doubt. But between his being soft on liberalism, apparently centrist, and under the gun of the rightwing mafia, I am not sanguine. I suspect that the old guerilla fighter, Buckley, has worked out a modus vivendi with the Neos—to speak bluntly, the NY Jews—and that Hollander is the compromise. Somehow I smell—no evidence—the supporters of our estimable Vice President in all of this. But Hollander has some good supporters, and I think you should stay cool, even if it kills you. If he gets it, some mutual friends may well convince him that you are to be placated—in which

case you may be able to swing some weight at the NEH. Business is business."

What now strikes me about this text, only a small part of which I have quoted, as well as about the very long letters that I received from Murray Rothbard, is the minute analysis that these texts bestowed on strategic problems. Contrary to expectations, the winner was Mrs. Cheney, someone whom most of the other candidates had not regarded as a front-runner. At the time of Gene's letter, Robert Hollander, a Dante scholar and professor of English at Princeton, seemed to have been the neoconservatives' preferred candidate, but he later dropped out of the running. The forces that stood behind him were probably the ones enumerated in Gene's letter, although there is little chance that if he had prevailed, Hollander and his supporters would have sought to "placate" me or allow me to throw around my "weight." For their part, Mrs. Cheney and her staff set out to placate the neoconservative power brokers but never as much as allowed me to referee a single project. The only NEH staffs that ever approved of any application from me were Democrats. Despite his tough, eloquent talk, Gene did not perceive how hostile the sides in the already raging conservative wars were by 1986. Nor did Mel understand the depth of the strife; he continued to grasp at the straw that "Podhoretz and Bill Buckley" would "encourage" the Reagan administration to appoint him as Librarian of Congress in 1987. I've no idea whether Mel got very far in the selection process, but I've no doubt that if he had made it through the first round, his old enemies would have taken the field against him once again.

It was Peter Stanlis who among the subjects of this chapter best grasped the tenacity of his adversaries, a skill that Mel, a truly gentle soul, utterly lacked. "We're in for a helluva fight with these

SOBs" was Peter's blunt assessment whenever he came back from a meeting with the NEH board. The two occasions when he told me that I would succeed in achieving a specific goal—my appointment at Rockford College and my winning of a Guggenheim Fellowship—had been accurately predicted. Significantly, my protector played critical but hard-to-trace roles in both situations.

I have known two Peters since the early 1970s. One is a bookish archivist who for as long as he has been my friend has been hard of hearing, a problem that has grown worse with age. Peter also enjoys "punishing" those he talks to with inept word plays; he now even seems proud of the "unfunny jokes" that he has accumulated over the decades. When Peter's beloved wife Eleanor, a distinguished violinist, died unexpectedly five years ago, we all thought that Peter would fall apart. The two had been inseparable, and they had known each other since attending college together at Middlebury. But Peter rallied and eventually remarried. His new wife is a former librarian at Rockford College whom I recall from my years in Rockford as being handsome and gracious.

The second Peter, whom I value even more highly than the writer on Burke, Frost, and eighteenth-century English culture, is a remarkably tough fellow. He is someone who can look at difficult or unexpected situations without distorting emotion or sentimentality. His lifelong tirade against Rousseau, the thinker who raised pity to the essence of morality, reflects his gloomy worldview. Although Peter has never had any use for the Puritans, who over several generations exchanged a belief in total depravity for a faith in basic human goodness, his own thinking is starkly Augustinian in the most unreconstructed sense. I have never known anyone who has been so thoroughly on guard against human depravity. Peter identifies this primal defect in our natures with the lust for power, a trait for which he is always on the lookout in his enemies. (He has been right in his moral judgments more often than I care to recall.)

Of all my allies in the struggle against the neoconservative ascendancy, Peter grasped the enormousness of the Old Right's problems earliest and best. He never entertained the vain hope that war could be avoided, and he assumed from the opening bell that our side would be fighting "with our backs to the ropes." In what has been called "the conservative wars of the '80s," Peter never thought that his enemies' philosophical ignorance was the reason they were trying to marginalize our side. His explanation followed from his reading of the temperamental Puritan Irving Babbitt: namely, that those who were stepping on our toes loved power and mistook their *libido dominandi* for the imposition of "moderation" and humanitarian agendas. For Peter there was no way that one could separate intellectual from moral virtues. His main cognitive limitation here may have been his inability to feel empathy for those he was forced to oppose. Once, while listening to him lace into "the politicians," meaning the neoconservatives, I was tempted to ask: Granted, they hate our guts, but aren't they motivated by fears similar to ours? At that point Peter told me that Gertrude Himmelfarb, whose dislike for me I never doubted, had assumed that I was a "German Catholic" who was only pretending to have come from a Jewish refugee family. Although her assumption startled me, it suggested that Peter's colleague on the NEH board obsessed about German Catholic anti-Semitism. Such a threat may now be a silly anachronism, but it had been a real concern for my ancestors as well as for those of Professor Himmelfarb. People may suffer from atavistic fears that complicate social and professional relations. But one must take those fears into account if one is trying to understand their personalities.

In Peter's defense, it should be said that he possesses what my wife Mary calls a "bottom-line personality." He tries to confront nasty situations as they arise, without dwelling on long-range causes. In this sense he is like Mary, a natural dog trainer who eschews speculation about "traumas" when she deals with unruly canine behavior. Peter, too, takes a consequentialist approach to addressing dysfunctional behavior. Thus, he showed no interest when I brought up the possible sociological reasons for the suspiciousness and intriguing that he encountered among his NEH colleagues. "That's their problem, not mine," was his usual retort to my futile clarifications.

Once, he brought to our home in Rockford some of his cousins who were visiting from Peter's native state of New Jersey. They had just returned from an excursion to a Lithuanian historical society in Chicago, which has the largest concentration of Lithuanian Americans of any city in the country. Peter's female cousin was full of details about how the Soviets had mistreated her ancestral nation. She lamented that over a million Lithuanians had been killed or disappeared into Soviet labor camps since 1940, and that their country had been handed over to Russian settlers whom Stalin had brought in to replace the earlier settlers. Peter listened pensively and then offered this comment: "They should have chosen their homeland more carefully. Now they have to deal with their Soviet conquerors." That was the most I ever heard Peter say against the Soviets and their tyranny. Never did he allow himself to descend into ethnic whining; and while he assumed in the language of Genesis that "man is bad from his youth," he worried less about the broad problem of evil than about its specific consequences in our lives. This tendency reminds me of Woody Allen's film *Hannah and Her Sisters*, in which the gloomy Swede played by Max von Sydow observes apropos of a documentary about Auschwitz: "The surprising thing is that such things happen as rarely as they do."

I met Christopher Lasch for the first time at a lecture that he gave at Case Western Reserve in 1969. It was the height of the Vietnam War, and I was an assistant professor in the history department. His remarks were centered on the U.S.'s responsibility for our bad relations with the Soviets. He made repeated references to a book he had written on the American intervention against the Bolshevik takeover of Russia in 1919, which Lasch considered the origin of our clashes with the Soviet Union. Lasch's remarks fitted in with the dominant anti-Americanism of the historical profession, and I associated his presence with certain setbacks that would soon befall me. In the following year my contract at Case Western Reserve was not renewed, and although a financial shortfall was cited as the official reason, I suspected that my older colleagues did nothing to save my skin because I was known on campus as a "Nixon Republican."

Lasch was teaching at a hotbed of the New Left, the University of Rochester history department, which was chaired by a self-described Stalinist, Gene Genovese. I immediately regarded him as persona non grata. My chairman, Jack J. Roth, who had hired me, was a friend of Lasch's, whom he had met while both were at Roosevelt University. I thought that Jack, whom I always suspected of being a closet, nonvoting Republican, was parading his friendship with a lunatic in order to ingratiate himself with our leftist colleagues. My diatribes against Lasch in conversations with Jack were an excessive reaction I now regret.

But my dislike for his friend only increased when I went to Rochester the following year as a candidate for an associate professorship. I came as Genovese's favored candidate; unfortunately, by then he and Lasch had fallen out over questions of departmental governance. Lasch never came to any of my scheduled interviews or to my very long, awkwardly delivered presentation on historiography, but he lurked behind the scenes as a vaporous, malign presence. He lined up votes against me that were then directed toward my rival candidate, who won in a squeaker. The setback that I suffered was so devastating that my career never really recovered. Not even the scheming that caused me to lose a graduate professorship at Catholic University of America seventeen years later did as much harm to me as Lasch caused in a single afternoon of conversations. The post at Rochester was in the scholarly field in which I was then publishing; it was in a prestigious department, membership in which would have opened other professional doors; and at twenty-nine I would have been young enough to take full advantage of my appointment. Within a year, moreover, the job market would collapse, and I was forced to work for several years as an educational administrator in New Jersey before landing an academic position at Rockford College. Although I was grateful for that berth, it did not compare to what I had lost because of Lasch's politicking.

Nonetheless, twenty years later Lasch—whom like most everyone I came to call "Kit"—and I became friends, to the point that he would openly discuss what had happened at the time of my interview. He had been genuinely concerned about what he saw as the highhanded way in which Gene was dealing with his duties as chairman, and he feared that Gene was trying to fill the junior professorships in the department with handpicked vassals. This possibility had dawned on me during my interview, and I told Kit that he might have been justified in his anxieties. It was entirely possible that out of gratitude and youthful enthusiasm I would have been what my Stalinist chairman Gene was looking for: an indisputable academic conservative who could be counted on to rally to his benefactor. In any case, I was willing to consider Kit's position because he admitted to what he had done—and he did so with regret in light of our later friendship. His behavior compares favorably to that of other, more powerful political enemies who have accused me of madness when I found their fingerprints on guns that had been fired at me. Kit never lied to me about his previous unfriendliness, which in his case was morally motivated.

The first time we met again face-to-face was at a conference held in 1990 at Elizabethtown College. By then I greatly admired his work on the therapeutic state (his magnum opus dealing with this vast subject, *The True and Only Heaven*, was about to be published by Norton), and a thematically related project that I would eventually pursue was taking shape in my head. The conference, on the future of community, had been arranged by the board of *Telos* magazine. When Kit got around to speaking about "scientific" administration as a threat to cultural identities, I found myself strongly seconding his remarks. But he also had a tendency to appeal to the consciousness of "real people," whom managerial government had supposedly marginalized. Claes Ryn, who was also present, criticized Kit for his "romantic populism," whereupon a firestorm erupted. Kit taunted Claes as an "elitist," a description that fitted and still fits this soft-spoken Nordic gentleman who appears everywhere in elegant attire. Claes retorted that you can't escape from elites; you get them no matter what, because the "people" have no sense of self-government. Indeed they want others to look after their needs.

I was caught in the middle in more than one way. The two disputants were both friends; and although I agreed with Claes that we ought to resist the impulse to romanticize the "people," Lasch had a certain populace in mind to which his designation undoubtedly applied. His rugged German ancestors who had settled in Nebraska as farmers, and the working-class families whom he contrasted to the sybaritic cosmopolites in his last book, *Revolt of the Elites* (1995), instantiate the "real people"—that is, those whom Lasch wished to re-empower. The question might be raised whether "the real people" form anything approaching a significant demographic part of today's America—or whether they exist for the most part as an idealized memory. But such a picture of the "people" informed Kit's populist conceptions. The good types who redeemed his dualistic universe were often the progenitors of the Catholic blue-collar working families that I can still vaguely recall from the 1950s. These families were marked by multiple offspring and by wives who prepared their husbands' lunch pails. Lasch's evocation of the females in his ideal but perhaps archaic nuclear family caused the feminist Susan Faludi to designate him as the "leading American sexist of the '90s."

I was puzzled by the mindset at the *New York Times* and *New York Review of Books* when their editors presented Kit after his death in 1994 as an archetypically leftist social critic. By then Lasch might have been moving to the right of Pat Buchanan on many social issues, despite the obvious fact that he retained his lifelong hatred of consumer capitalism, a trait that he might have inherited from his socialist mother. His devotion to a nonmainstream form of socialism was something he discussed with me after I had learned about it from his contributions to the Catholic, anticapitalist fortnightly *New Oxford Review*. Despite his Presbyterian affiliation and general theological skepticism, Kit earnestly read the English Catholic distributists and the essays of the Catholic advocate for labor, Dorothy Day. His project was to find a religiously based communitarianism that could serve as an alternative to multinational capitalism. This communal identity would focus on service to one's family and neighbors, and it would supposedly take everyone's mind off consumption and the false idea of "Progress." No popular idol exasperated Kit as deeply as the American fixation on making everything better, even at the cost of abolishing stable institutions. This theme is a leitmotif running through his early work, when he was still identifiably leftist, until *Revolt of the Elites*. His posthumously printed writings, edited by his daughter Elisabeth Lasch-Quinn, confirm the impression created by what Kit brought out during his all too short life.

Unlike my other well-known correspondents, I have managed to preserve only one letter from Kit. Other missives came before this one, which is dated March 22, 1990, from his home in Pittsford, New York, but those were mostly scribbled responses to my occasional queries. In this typed letter, Kit pours scorn on *Commentary* magazine, a publication that, he writes, "I never read if I can help it." In a recent issue Midge Decter had slammed him for contributing to the dissolution of middle-class morality, a charge that I brought to his attention in a humorous way. Kit, who personified an old-fashioned Presbyterian way of life, took umbrage at the slight: "That is the first time I've been attacked as an advocate of sexual promiscuity. It's kind of nice to be attacked from the right for a change. It's the attacks from the left that still bother me."

Two thoughts flashed through my mind as I read these observations. First, on the basis of what Kit had recently published—soon expanded on in *The True and Only Heaven*—all traditional distinctions between "left" and "right" had broken down. Since both sides now believed in consumerism, Progress, and centralized government, it was misleading to go on drawing critical distinctions between them. Two, if Midge Decter really knew what Lasch believed, she would have attacked him from the left rather than the right. What she had mistakenly attributed to him were the countercultural stances that had come out of the '60s, positions that in fact he had never taken.

Another reason I've only one of Lasch's letters is that by 1993 he was writing to his friends collectively about his deteriorating health—specifically, about the spread of his cancer. I found the topic inexpressibly painful, since my own wife was then dying of cancer, so I probably discarded the communications after having looked at them. Kit's unhappy fate still makes me think about a lunch at a local restaurant that he had with me and two of my colleagues when he was visiting Elizabethtown. On that occasion Kit smoked a cigarette and ordered a dark beer in order to make the point that "people are too damned concerned about living forever." These gestures might have been intended to make a statement about health-conscious yuppies; I myself could have been one of the "health nuts" whom Kit was trying to shock when he smoked and drank at lunch. By then (alas) his life was coming to an end—sooner than any of us realized.

I first met his longtime and long-estranged colleague Gene Genovese at the December 1970 gathering of the American Historical Association in Boston. I was not only Gene's copanelist for a discussion of new directions in Marxism; I was also interviewed by him in his hotel suite. Our conversation was supposed to center on my eligibility for the aforementioned opening in his history department. But I recall little or nothing about our discussion of professional matters. My first impression was that Gene, who appeared in a tailored suit and was plainly accustomed to sumptuous living, was a strange-looking socialist revolutionary. My second impression was that his favorite subject was the American Right. In fact, he spent the better part of our half-hour meeting pointing out the connection between the current positions of *National Review* editors to where they had stood while they were still on the Marxist Left. His observations were so acute that I found myself drawing on them while preparing my recent book on the American Right.

On the panel, Gene said nothing in his eloquent commentary that was reminiscent of a Marxist. I was pleased that he responded to my own remarks by stressing points of agreement. I had taken shots at a Jewish Marxist humanist who had exaggerated Marx's suffering at the hands of German anti-Semites. Marx, I noted, was raised in a Lutheran household, his own work abounds in unkind references to Jews, and if one wishes to embrace his historical teachings, there is no reason to dress them up with inflated reports about his victim status. Gene concurred with my judgment; but, as things turned out, we were rowing even then against the rising tide of victimology. I also remember that Gene and the English Communist Eric Hobsbawm, to whom he introduced me after the session, complained about the "exotica" that had crept into Marxist-Leninism. Young scholars were less interested in studying dialectical materialism than they were in glorifying the unspoiled virtues of non-Western peoples.

As I looked at these men, both dressed like Mr. Chips, I began to wonder what place would await them in that New Leftist landscape they were describing and bewailing. They were of course entirely correct in their observations, and in retrospect it seems to me that they had perceived the beginnings of the transition from the Marxist to the multicultural Left. The American Right, which still focused on a communist enemy, only glimpsed darkly what was then taking place at home. The foreign enemy on which they set their sights differed from the cultural forces that would occupy our public sector, media, and educational institutions. And that internal foe would be dangerous because of the relentless crusade it would wage against Western civilization and its defining social and moral institutions. Within ten years of my conversation with these gentlemanly Marxists, the advocates of upheaval would be pursuing the same ends everywhere in the Western world. By then they, too, would be attired in Brooks Brothers suits or their European equivalents. The passion for "exotica" observed by Hobsbawm was the portent of worse things to come.

My next meeting with Gene took place during the morning of my interview at Rochester, when he and his spouse Betsey picked me up in my hotel room and took me to breakfast. I carried away positive impressions of these hosts, and particularly of Gene's wife (who passed away in January 2007). Although they mentioned that the history department at Rochester had become the scene of some infighting, they sketched a future in which this would no longer be the case. It was never made clear to me how this happy prospect would be realized, but the thought of being in the same department with Gene, who had been featured in the national press as one of America's most brilliant historians, caused my doubts to melt away. Besides, his wife, who was a Simon-Morgenthau on her mother's side, pronounced French exquisitely, and Betsey (whose full name was Elizabeth) struck me as a classy and attractive young woman. Why should I care if they chose to call themselves Marxists or faced a strife-ridden department? In any case, Betsey assured me that at SUNY-Binghamton, where she was teaching, quarreling had also raged in the recent past.

When I was taken to meet the Rochester faculty, a professor whose specialty was the English civil war informed me that Stephen Tonsor had preceded me as an interviewee. Having looked over the department, Tonsor had expressed misgivings about leaving his post at the University of Michigan. "He was a Republican and I didn't want the guy even if Gene did," was the professor's remark to me as

I left his office. His unadorned opinion about nonleftists made me feel less than hopeful. At Case Western, it had been held against me that I had admitted to voting for Richard Nixon in 1968. I also knew that when Gene had been at Rutgers University in the 1960s, Nixon had made critical remarks about Genovese's open support of the Vietcong. But Gene had never held this act against the former vice president, and in 1972, although still an avowed Marxist, he was accused of having voted for Nixon. Several years later, I met Gene's former colleague, the Renaissance historian Marvin Becker. He was still seething over "Gene's phony leftism." By then I too had begun to wonder about the authenticity of his revolutionary radicalism, which I explained years later in an essay for *Telos* by arguing that Gene was an antibourgeois elitist trying to fit into American academia.

The problem with fitting Gene into my conception of the academic Left is that he did not resemble the three types of leftists I had previously encountered—and whom I have been encountering ever since. The first two types were Jewish but divided easily into two categories. One, the representatives of which were predominantly Central European in ancestry, were conspicuously bookish and spent considerable energy working to make the world conform to a Marxist scheme of reality. Such leftists were usually multilingual and typically shared my interest in German philosophy. But they also slavishly supported the Soviets and had a blind spot when it came to the many acts of mass murder committed by Communist regimes. Although themselves the products of elitist humanistic educations, they also professed great love for the unwashed, a group whom they rarely dealt with. I would have greatly enjoyed the company of such leftists except for one source of friction. I found their denials or whitewashing of the most gruesome tyranny in modern history, equaled only by the crimes of the Third Reich, to be inexpressibly repulsive.

The second, and more tedious, type of academic leftists was composed of New York Jews of Eastern European origin who were fixated on one overriding fear: anti-Semitism. They seemed to experience this danger in proportion to how far they traveled outside of the New York metropolitan area. They were and are the most insecure group I have known, and their prominence in today's elite history departments testifies to the decrepitude of an older Christian establishment they easily replaced. In this case I can locate no conceivable fit between the radicalism of these radicals and anything that connects to classical Marxism. In preparing my book on the post-Marxist Left, I had in mind among others these denizens of the academic fantasy world. But I would also note that the neurotic Jewish intellectuals under discussion have formed an exceedingly harmonious relationship with the yuppie Left. The enablers of Type Two now abound everywhere, and whenever Type Two members are moved to scream "fascist," "racist," and "anti-Semite," droves of non-Jewish academics can be expected to rush to their defense and call for therapeutic and political action.

The third type of academic leftist, the PC gentile, is the one whom I have come to like the least. While Type Two consists of Woody Allen–like neurotics who think that they are protecting themselves and their group against a pervasive external gentile enemy, Type Three is arrogant and suicidal. In Europe and the U.S., Type Three representatives coddle or excuse Islamic terrorists, and they regard their own civilization as so worthless or so evil that they seek to "enrich" it by bringing in never-ending supplies of Third World immigrants. The faculty and administrators influenced by this persuasion are eager to remove all references to Christmas from school programs but never stop celebrating Kwanzaa and jabbering about Ramadan. They also treat Martin Luther King Jr. as a replacement for the vanished savior in their old religion, and they go into high gear during black and women's history months, pointing out our continued sins of omission in dealing with these designated victims.

As a leftist, Gene was so different from all of these types that it was impossible to relate him to any of them, except for his occasional associations with Type One. Like those particular leftists, and like former Communists James Burnham and Will Herberg, his interest in Marxism seemed largely cerebral. Perhaps in trying to make sense of the present age, Gene simply adopted a fashionable model for historical interpretation that was associated with intellectuals, one that combined "scientific" claims with apparent humanitarian concern. Over the years, as I have studied his monographs and essays, starting with his early *The World the Slaveholders Made* (1969), I have never stopped noticing how much of a structural conservative, in the nineteenth-century sense, Gene has always been. His obligatory references to oppressed black slaves and the Marxist dialectic notwithstanding, his works are essentially tributes to precapitalist societies based on hierarchy and a Christian sense of order. His overtly traditionalist later writings, such as *The Southern Tradition: The Achievement and Limitations of An American Conservatism* (1994) and the massive volume that he copublished with his wife in 2005, *The Mind of the Master Class: History and Faith in the Southern Slaveholders' Worldview*, are not significantly different in their interpretive framework or moral assumptions from what Gene produced as a putative Stalinist.

His most conventionally leftist book remains, in my opinion, *From Rebellion to Revolution* (1979), a slim volume that Gene might have done to appease his mounting critics on the left who found him insufficiently sensitive. In this work he attributes to black slaves a consciousness that arose independently of their capricious masters. He tries to trace among these slaves the emergence of a revolutionary élan that might have resulted in class war. More dramatically than his other writings, *From Rebellion to Revolution* dwells in excruciating detail on the physical suffering of the slave class. This last theme had been of special interest to University of California-Berkeley historian Kenneth Stampp, an outspoken critic of Gene's previous analysis of the slave economy.

I once discussed my perceptions about Gene's relation to the Left with a longtime correspondent, Aileen Kraditor, who knew him while both were associated with the Communist Party. Aileen argued that Gene was expressing immaculately Communist historical views when he treated black slaves as reflecting the worldview of the Southern planter class. Gene was applying the view of the Italian Communist theorist Antonio Gramsci, who had expounded the notion that the ruling class typically imposes a "hegemonic ideology" that paralyzes the revolutionary potential of those they oppress. The slaves acted and thought like their masters, in Gene's narrative, because their minds and bodies belonged to their masters.

In spite of the plausibility of this argument, I never believed that Gene was simply adapting a Gramscian form of Marxism, a theory that in any case is not orthodox Marxism but rather a view of social consciousness based on Hegelian philosophy more than historical materialism. What Gene did with the theory looked very different from what had been done with it by neo-Marxists, and particularly by feminists and black nationalists. More conventional leftists poured wrath on the master class, but Gene admired the "mind of the slaveholder," and he devoted long respectful disquisitions to those Southern Presbyterian theologians who had defended the South's peculiar institution.

A friend quipped that after Gene had returned to his ancestral Catholic faith in 1996 and had begun denouncing Communist atrocities, his politics began to slide leftward. As long as he had presented himself as a Stalinist and Gramscian, he could afford to treat the Southern planter class sympathetically and play up Southern Agrarians as perceptive critics of world capitalism. Once, however, Gene had become a regular fixture of the establishment Right and developed friendships with neoconservatives, he supposedly had to monitor his right-wing sympathies more carefully. Given the neoconservatives' funding of and prominence in The Historical Society, a nonradical alternative to the American Historical Association that he and Betsey launched in 1998, the idea that Gene was put under restraints that had not operated in the past seems correct.

But the continuity between his past and present convictions is still sufficiently evident that it would be difficult to describe him as having swerved in an entirely different direction since the early '90s. His recent work on the religious outlook of the slaveholders shows continued empathy for its subjects; and despite his Catholic practices, Gene does not hide his theological affinity for Southern Calvinists, about whom he writes with obvious respect. At the very neoconservative National Association of Scholars annual gathering several years ago, at which I happened to be present, Gene delivered a speech after having been given an award. His remarks were a glowing defense of Old Southern virtues and pieties, and at least by implication, this Italian-American from Bayside, Brooklyn, took aim at the current conservative movement for repudiating its Southern heritage. From the faces of his listeners, it seemed that his observations went over about as well as a ringing endorsement of Hamas would have.

Exemplifying his persistent attempt to balance countervailing sentiments and loyalties was a conversation I had with Gene when I took my eldest daughter, as a high-school senior, to visit the University of North Carolina campus in 1987. Gene was staying in a studio apartment above the garage of the home of John Shelton Reed, the sociologist of Southern culture, while on a research trip to Chapel Hill. At dinner I noticed that Gene lived far more abstemiously than he had when I had been at Rochester sixteen years earlier. He had given up cigars, drank wine to prevent high blood pressure rather than as a pleasure, and avoided foods with transfat (long before yuppies had begun to rage over this dietary indulgence).

But the old Gene came through as soon as he started talking about politics, and especially about recent Eastern European political history. Although my interlocutor did not mind that the Soviets had occupied Rumania in 1944 and then stayed there, or that they decided to bestow on their new subjects the blessing of socialism, he was bothered by how shabbily they had treated King Michael, the last royal ruler of Rumania. Despite the king's previous opposition to the German occupation and his willingness to cooperate with the Soviets up to a point, the Soviets had unceremoniously forced Michael into exile in 1946. Gene viewed this as a lost opportunity to combine two opposing principles, revolutionary socialism and monarchism, into a single system of government. I thereupon found myself asking what practical difference it would have made if the Soviet occupiers of Rumania had kept the monarch around as a figurehead. Countries like Sweden, Belgium, Holland, and England had reigning monarchs but had long ceased to be traditional societies by bourgeois Victorian standards. Indeed, it might be argued that by retaining the outward appearance of monarchical continuity, one bestowed on radical social engineering a semblance of convention. On balance, this anachronism contributed nothing positive to social conservation.

But these were not the arguments that Gene wanted to hear. He was still searching for a middle ground between the two poles of his anticapitalist attitude: namely, the precapitalist, hierarchical society shaped by the relationship between *padroni* and *clienti*, and imperfectly approximated by the world that the slaveholders built; and the forced march into postcapitalist socialism. Rarely have I encountered anyone who has worked so arduously to reconcile such plainly contradictory positions.

Until the late 1980s, the man whom Gene had supported for the post of NEH chairman, M. E. Bradford, had been at most an occasional acquaintance of mine. I had run across him on those rare occasions when I attended the Philadelphia Society's annual meetings, then typically held in Chicago, and I recall that someone had pointed out his burly figure soon after the election of Ronald Reagan as the heir apparent to the NEH chairmanship. Mel's failure to obtain that post and the way it was denied to him deeply affected my political attitudes. I wrote a letter of reference for him in response to the urging of Peter Stanlis. And though I opposed the NEH as a constitutionally dubious boondoggle set up to feather the nests of government administrators exchanging favors with prestigious universities, I felt that if such an institution could do any possible good it might be in providing a Southern Agrarian with a high-profile job. Alas, that was not to be; Mel spent the remainder of his life trying in vain to win a compensatory prize for the big fish that had gotten away.

It was only after I had relocated to Washington in the summer of 1986 that Mel and I became close friends. Mel was always looking for some excuse to come to the nation's capital, such as having to attend a meeting of the Fulbright board, where he could shake hands and knock on doors in an effort to get his stalled political career jump-started. These endeavors did not bring him any benefit; worse, his trips from his home in suburban Dallas to Washington National Airport probably contributed to the mounting health problems caused by his excessive weight.

By the fall of 1986, Mel was also writing essays for my monthly journal. I called upon his services as often as I did primarily for three reasons. One, he had enthusiastically assisted me in my recent unsuccessful bid for the post that he himself had been denied. Two, I felt that a common destiny—shared enemies—united us. And three, I liked the historical view that came through in his work. Like Gene, Mel sounded like a structural conservative, a term that obviously meant more to me than it did to him, given my European intellectual historical interests. Mel's task in *The Reactionary Imperative* (1989), *A Worthy Company* (1982), and in his other collections of essays, which was to locate the Southern planter class in a specific structure of authority and to define its worldview, seemed to me a perfectly sensible exercise. It might have been impossible to "recapture," in the sense of reactivating, the values of "our ancestors"; nonetheless, one could trace a connection between what they had thought and the kind of society in which they had lived. And even if one granted that Thomas Jefferson, Patrick Henry, and John Taylor of Caroline were influenced by the social-contract theory of government that gained currency during the Enlightenment, such prominent men also had to filter "enlightened" notions through their everyday experiences as landowners in a manorial society. Perhaps there was a disconnect between their social position and declarations of Christian faith and their natural-rights statements; or else perhaps the dominant class managed somehow to synthesize different and apparently contradictory elements of their understandings of government and societies.

Unlike the Straussians, a group of scholars with whom I was

already then quarreling, Mel, like Gene, looked at social-historical contexts in trying to make sense of what the American founding generation had actually believed. Through Mel's books, as the justly famous historian Forrest McDonald once observed, one could learn what secularists were working to hide, namely, that most of the Southerners among the founding generation were in fact devout Protestants. If such figures were religious skeptics, one would have trouble discovering that from perusing their letters and diaries.

Mel never denied that a certain filial pietism informed his judgments about his favorite historical actors. "I've always taken a Roman approach to historical greatness," he explained to me, and he made place for "enthymēsiss," his favorite Greek term, in his characterizations of particular figures. As best I could figure out, Mel was referring to the *enthumemata* in Aristotle's *Rhetoric*, a speaking device that is meant to appeal to the heart as well as the head. He also sounded Aristotelian in his insistence on the need for epic figures as a guide for later generations. Not surprisingly, the figures whom Mel showcased in his historical writings were usually landowning farmers, a fact that fits in well with his preferred and by then archaic model of American life.

Although much of Mel's published work was on the literature of the American Southwest, he was clearly interested in defending a particular "vision of order," to quote the term of his fellow Southerner Richard Weaver. His distaste for Lincoln reflected not only his bitterness about the Civil War, a struggle in which his ancestors had fought on the losing side, but also his revulsion for the "god terms" that Lincoln had invoked in prosecuting a bloody internecine war. Like Burke and other European conservatives, Mel wanted no part of those "armed doctrines" which have been appealed to by universal revolutionaries. Mel's quarrel with Lincoln was based to some extent on the central role that our sixteenth president had assumed in a global democratic hagiography.

As a thinker, Mel stressed the need to anchor political beliefs in both concrete experiences and communal practices. To the argument that actual traditions could be oppressive for some people, his response would be that such objectors could move to New York or San Francisco. And even if some traditions were truly noxious, he would say, it was impossible to imagine a society functioning in their absence that had not descended into dictatorship or anarchy. Although Mel viewed the civil-rights movement as a disaster that had brought federal administrators into every aspect of our civic and personal lives, I never heard him speak ill about blacks as a group. Like many Southerners of his generation—including those who, like him, had moved from Oklahoma to Texas—he had simply taken a segregated way of life for granted.

Nonetheless, in contrast to most leftists of my acquaintance, Mel, his wife Marie, and his son Doug all got along exceedingly well with people of color whenever they came into contact with them. One of Mel's friends was the black humanist scholar William B. Allen at Michigan State, with whom he happily arranged colloquia for Liberty Fund. It was in connection to Professor Allen that I heard Mel make the comment that the basic flaw of the "old system"—whether that meant slavery or segregation was not clear—was "that it kept down those black people who could have made a social contribution." I mention this remark because the attempts to depict Mel as a fanatical racist have been as inexcusably malicious as everything else his critics have said about him. I am also puzzled why "traditionalists" who have attacked Mel for being insensitive to segregation and for supporting George Wallace in the presidential race in 1968 do not show a comparable indignation over "moderate Republicans" who endorse gay marriage and late-term abortion. Why are these issues less central as moral concerns for Mel's detractors than were his reservations about the civil-rights movement in the 1960s? Dare I suggest the obvious answer that these "traditionalists" are applying the politically correct standards of the day?

One side of Mel's personality may continue to puzzle some of his acquaintances. Although hardly reluctant to make statements that were likely to draw fire, he would quickly withdraw from the hostilities he occasioned once they commenced. Mel looked at provocative declarations as opportunities for discussion, and when they became something more, he was upset by the ensuing strife. This may be attributed to two of his characteristics: the desire to raise professorial questions, as he did to brilliant effect as a professor at the University of Dallas, and his naturally sweet disposition. Mel was not made of the stern stuff that he admired in Confederate commanders. Although he had served as a naval officer in some previous incarnation, he was not cut out for belligerence. A family friend had once observed to me that while "Marie, who comes from mountain folk, would tear her enemy's eyes out, Mel had no stomach for such stuff."

This became particularly clear when I asked Mel to prepare a review essay for *The World and I* on the most recent collection of occasional pieces by his adversary Norman Podhoretz. I certainly had evil designs when I commissioned this assignment, and I expected Mel to be equal to the task, particularly since he had told me that he considered the anthology essays "so much puffery." What came back, however, was something that looked like a literary exercise that might have been submitted at a private school for Southern girls circa 1840. It oozed politeness and only hinted at critical observations, which were never directly stated. When I asked Mel why he had pulled punches, he answered: "I didn't want to seem impolite, particularly after what had happened." Although "what had happened" was that Mel's reputation had been blackened beyond repair by the associates of Norman Podhoretz, if not by this publicist directly, Mel did not want to reveal hard feelings after having suffered at someone else's hands. He therefore bent over backward in order to mute his reservations about a book that offended him.

Of the multiple subjects of this chapter, Robert Nisbet (1913–96) was the one whom I knew well for the shortest period of time. Despite his generous favors toward me, such as reviewing *The Search for Historical Meaning* in *National Review* in exhaustive detail and exerting himself to obtain for me a graduate professorship at CUA, I only became personally acquainted with Bob during the last ten years of his life. By then his reputation as a social theorist was long established, and he and his wife Caroline had left New York, where he had been Albert Schweitzer Professor of Humanities at Columbia University, to move into a comfortable apartment on Wisconsin Avenue in Washington. Although he had some connection to the American Enterprise Institute, he was not there often, and he expressed shock in his conversations with me that AEI fellows were expected to "bring in their own money." As a formerly lavishly paid academic, Bob could never quite grasp why think tanks did not honor their fellows in the same way as did Columbia. But he did show considerable interest in our monthly. He wrote for several issues, including a long essay on the British constitutional historian James Bryce, and he came to at least one of our board meetings as an honorary advisor. It seems that our publisher had been his comrade-in-arms on the Pacific island of

Sampan during World War II, and Bob seemed loath to "disappoint my old war buddy Mort."

One of the oddities of my knowing him is that I never saw Bob outside of formal social and professional situations. This was the case despite the fact that I am in possession of many typed letters from him, all of which were sent from his apartment in Northwest Washington to my office just a few miles away. I sat a few feet away from him when Bob received an Ingersoll Prize from the Rockford Institute in Chicago in 1985, and I vaguely recall meeting him when he came to Rockford to address the newly formed Rockford Institute in the late 1970s. His speech at that time was a sulfurous diatribe directed against public administration, and it drew an extended comparison between FDR's New Deal and the fascist experiment begun in Italy in the 1920s. What impressed me most was how elegantly attired the speaker was and how well his tall slender frame and strikingly handsome face would have suited the movie actors whom I had seen in the 1950s. (He was, after all, from Southern California.) His Ingersoll Prize address was a more subdued exercise in social criticism; and when in 1988 Bob was awarded the Jefferson Lecture by the National Endowment for the Humanities, his remarks exemplified the kind of avoidance-of-conflict tone that I would not have identified with him ten years earlier.

As often as I met Bob in formal situations and as often as I spoke to him over the phone, I never visited his dwelling or he mine. Although I was told that this was because Bob was a "private person," I doubt that was the entire story. Both Bob and his wife were known to be gregarious, and from all reports, they often received and entertained their offspring and extended family. What seems likely, on the basis of my later communications with Caroline, is that Bob was ailing for some time with leukemia, from which he finally passed on after I moved from Washington. Since he had to rally his strength for social encounters, he did not want to overtax himself with unnecessarily strenuous festivities.

Everything about Robert Nisbet was *bon ton*. He kept to himself unless he was properly prepared, as the French say, "de recevoir le monde." His political tastes, as I observed in an essay for *Policy Review* in 1986 that dealt with his book *Conservatism*, reflected an aesthetic more than ideological point of view. While Bob exalted the personalities of eighteenth-century Tories and early-nineteenth-century counterrevolutionaries, he had no patience for religious enthusiasts; and despite his Protestant background and values, he disliked American fundamentalists with particular intensity. His recurrent nightmare was that these "tasteless people" and the constantly expanding administrative state would make some kind of deal, whence would emerge a combination of a social-engineering government and a latter-day approximation of Oliver Cromwell's commonwealth.

Such a nightmare would not come to pass, but from Bob's point of view, all ranters were kindred spirits, even if their nostrums and the content of their hysterics varied with time and place. I have always felt that his disconcerting stand in favor of abortion rights did not betoken any interest in "women's issues." It is unimaginable that Bob ever thought about such things. As Brad Lowell Stone stresses in his Nisbet biography, it is difficult to overstate his subject's distaste for the Religious Right. Bob clearly did not view the adherents of that Right as "traditionalist communitarians," as opposed to a cheering gallery for Big Government. Although an advocate of state restrictions on abortion and of the treatment of late-term abortion as homicide, I fully share Bob's misgivings about the Religious Right as a promoter of government overreach. Whether such enthusiasts also encourage speaking in tongues or the handling of snakes concerns me far less than it did Robert Nisbet.

Despite his invectives against the "national state," by which he meant the federal administration and its subordinate bureaucracy at the state level, and despite his production of an entire monograph, *The Present Age* (1988), devoted to this encroaching danger, Bob thoroughly admired Richard Nixon, a president who certainly added to governmental growth. This was because friendship meant a great deal to him; and although his views often diverged from theirs, he always esteemed the former president and Gertrude Himmelfarb as personal friends. Such relations functioned independently of Bob's political worldview, which translated as small-government, old-fashioned Republicanism.

Bob had no use for American crusades for democracy, but he also thought that the Second World War and the Cold War had been thrust upon us by historical circumstances. What bothered him was that even these necessary struggles took place under the sponsorship of expansive ideologies, and in the case of the Second World War gave impetus to an administrative state that he had begun to attack as early as 1953 in *The Quest for Community*. At the same time, Bob managed to exclude from this judgment the state-expanding Richard Nixon. When I tried in vain to invite him to a dinner party that the former president was arranging, his response was: "No, I can't go. But please tell him that we are grateful for what he tried to do to save this republic." Although an admirer of Nixon's intelligence and a critic of most of his critics, I would be hard-pressed to find evidence that Nixon had "tried to save this republic."

One of Bob's many merits is that he understood his work as a sociologist and social theorist to be an "art form." When Transaction publisher Irving Louis Horowitz asked me about twenty years ago to write an introduction to a new edition of Nisbet's *Sociology as an Art Form* (1976), I found that the argument of this work seemed infinitely more sensible than the views of "scientific" sociologists and political "scientists," whose number-crunching has always seemed to me a new form of medieval numerology. Bob observed that the reason most social scientists have been attracted to Marx and his historical theory has less to do with Marx's "scientific" content than his powerful appeal to the imagination and moral sense. And the reason that postwar academics had "rediscovered" Marx and Marxism was not their quantifying methodology but rather the idealistic rhetoric that abounded in the "Paris Manuscripts" and in the other texts authored by the young Marx.

One of the frequently posed questions about Bob's oeuvre is why he devoted considerable energy to popularizing the thesis, in *History of the Idea of Progress* (1980), of the famous Berkeley professor Frederick Teggart. Bob used to joke that his friends "still can't figure out how I could be the author of that work." As best I can answer that question, Bob's sympathetic treatment of the notion of human advancement from Hellenistic culture and the primitive church onward, reaching its culminating point in various democratic revolutions, is not an exhortation to his own generation to imagine that everything is getting better in every way. It is hard to square such an interpretation with the portentous tone of *The Quest for Community* and *The Present Age*, two works separated by thirty-five years but offering equally harsh views about the Goliath steps of social engineering in the twentieth century.

Bob probably wrote his study at least partly as a tribute to a teacher who personified his professional outlook. He always looked upon Teggart as one of America's premier intellectual historians, someone whose lectures he had listened to with great care, and whose *Theory of History* (1925) Bob often referred to in conversation.

He believed that the idea of Progress, which Teggart had traced in his lectures and publications, was one of the mythic and conceptual foundations of our civilization. Although Bob's other works might call into question this particular notion, he warned against discounting the power of the *idea* of Progress. In *The Sociological Tradition* (1967), he notes that even the counterrevolutionaries of the early nineteenth century carried with their Christian view of time a sense of human improvement in relation to the earlier era of paganism. This was the Augustinian legacy of the notion of a theocentric time moving toward a final age from a sinful pagan past. Moreover, the idea of Progress has typically featured a view of order extending from the past into the present. Only in its extreme form does this view result in the belief in a secular "golden age in the future." Indeed, "it was only when men become conscious of a long past, one held in common through ritual and then history and literature, that a consciousness of progressive movement from past to present became possible, a consciousness easily extrapolated to the future."

To whatever extent Bob defended the notion of Progress, it was as a pattern of civilization and custom to which the present generation should regard itself as linked. He naturally resonated to my work on Hegel and the postwar American Right, which argued that historical consciousness defines a truly conservative worldview. In this book, I took up a theme that Bob had already discussed in 1980 in his work on Progress, the growing tendency to "disown the past." According to Bob, I had demonstrated how the deprecation of historical consciousness was now a conservative project, as self-styled conservatives railed against "historicism" as impeding the development of a politics of "abstract universals." Implicit in both of our works, but more explicitly present in *The Quest for Community*, is the view that a growing disjunction between past and present adds to the loss of historical continuity. Abstractions and utopian ideals about global, diverse communities may be all that is left in the growing social and cultural vacuum that marks the contemporary West.

I was recently brought back to these observations when I asked upper-level students in a politics and religion course whether the Amish and Mennonites, who are our neighbors in central Pennsylvania, are Catholics or Protestants. Those in the class who bothered to respond said "Catholic," but when I asked how they had arrived at that answer, my students could not explain. Despite their study of religion and their nominal membership in Protestant churches, they had absolutely no idea that Catholics and Protestants differ theologically. Given this ignorance, it is hard to figure out why some of them offered one uninformed answer rather than another. (From subsequent investigation I discovered that most of these students have made the honor list at our liberal-arts college.)

What unifies the subjects of this chapter? I believe that it is their rejection of the dominant American sense of social and moral Progress. At a time when the past was coming to be viewed as a source of bigotry and irrationality, these figures raised up models of order by looking backward. My friends held no brief for the growing stress on individual autonomy that one encounters in today's cultural industry. Even more politically incorrectly, they believed that without firm, inherited structures of authority, individuals would become the playthings of those who could manipulate their vanity and exploit their social and emotional fragility. None of these thinkers embraced the illusion that modern Americans were moving toward self-actualization in proportion to the breakdown of families and of once established communities.

Note that I developed or deepened my relationships with all of these dignitaries at a time when Ronald Reagan was providing verbal assurance that "America is back." Unlike others on what called itself the Right, none of these older friends blithely imagined that he was witnessing a "conservative revolution." The 1980s, or what they understood of them, had not changed much for the better, even if the occupant of the White House was praising "values" and speaking tough to the Soviets. All of these friends—perhaps especially an apparent Marxist, Gene Genovese—were keenly aware of the losses of the modern era, and of the vain and often shabby attempts made by the state and the market to compensate for them. They were less concerned about the much vaunted benefits of further change than they were about the consequences of those questionable changes in manners and morals which had taken place during their lives, changes that they viewed with mounting distrust. I cannot imagine that these prophets against Progress would think any differently about the present time. I mean the latest phase of our late modernity, the one in which I am now writing as a senior citizen about my teachers, and about the warnings against the worship of Progress that they passed on to me.

Acknowledgments

The construction of these memoirs is something I did after considerable prodding. It was Jeremy Beer and my wife Mary who pushed me into this project about three years ago. (I was then working on other more pressing assignments.) Without their encouragement, and in my wife's case, browbeating, I would not have signed a contract with ISI that obliged me to go through with the telling of my encounters. Mary, Jeremy, Dan McCarthy, John Lukacs, W. Wesley McDonald, Wilfred M. McClay, David S. Brown, and Dr. Alice Baumgart all looked at the changing and sometimes tortuous drafts of the various chapters, and they renewed my enthusiasm for a task that I periodically tired of.

The first completed draft was so lifeless that I was about to chuck it, until my friends suggested ways of juicing up the narrative, by making it more personal and more anecdotal. Meanwhile my two eldest children, Barbara and Joey (both well into their thirties) expressed excitement about my intention but not necessarily about the finished work, which they never saw until it was published. My younger brother Dennis also enhanced my diligence, without knowing it, by stressing the honor that I was bestowing on our forbears by producing this work. For both of us, members of the same biological family, filial-pietism trumps most other virtues. The energetic assistance of ISI Books, and particularly of Chris Michalski and Jennifer Connolly, also kept me moving in a productive direction. And the polished quality of the final product owes much to the copy editing of Bill Kauffman, who is a gifted stylist, as his many books should make evident.

I would also like to mention a young gentleman (he may be among the last of his kind) Richard Spencer, with whom I've worked on a website, Taki's Top Drawer. Richard, who is a true Southern patrician, has been a sympathetic listener, and I have belabored him with my musings more often than I should have. I also drew solace from my conversations with my surviving, youngest aunt, May, who was my first heartthrob several eons ago. This aunt, whom I once regarded as the loveliest of all women but whom I could not have imagined myself being married to because of her advanced age (she was then 28) expressed the wish to see this book finished. As I told her, it was no pleasure to produce. Its revelations about my past and the need to rethink the suffering and death of others brought more unhappiness than fond reminiscences. Without the encouragement of others, I would never have completed these sometimes sad encounters.

Index

1999: Victory without War (Nixon), 133

A
Abzug, Bella, 29
Academy of Philosophy and Letters, 132
Adams, John, 120, 138
Adams, John Quincy, 138
Adenauer, Konrad, 109
Adler, Frank, 79, 81, 91
Adorno, Theodor, 47, 52, 53–55, 57, 58, 92
After Liberalism (Gottfried), 41, 87, 88, 105, 118, 120
Ahlstrom, Sidney, 28
Allen, William B., 195
Allen, Woody, 91, 177, 187
Allitt, Patrick, 98
American Cause, The, 130, 149

American Conservatism: An Encyclopedia (Frohnen et al.), viii
American Council for Judaism, 68
American Enterprise Institute (AEI), 197
American Heritage, 106
American Historical Association, 183, 190
American Political Science Association, xv
American Renaissance, 157
American Spectator, 133
Americanization, 113–15
Américanologie (Molnar), 98
America's Great Depression (Rothbard), 161
Anderson, John B., 143
Annenberg, Walter, 144–45
Anti-Defamation League, 100, 127

Aristotle, 10, 122, 128, 159, 194
Arnold, Matthew, 23
Ästhetische Kritik der Moderne (Luhr), 50
Augustine, 103, 202
Auschwitz, 127, 177
Ausmus, Harry, 67
Austria, 164
Austrian economics, 152
Austrian Perspective on the History of Economic Thought, An (Rothbard), 164
Austro-Hungarian army, 5
Authoritarian Personality, The (Adorno et al.), 54, 92
Authority and Its Enemies (Molnar), 99

B
Babbitt, Irving, 53, 176
Barth, Karl, 111
Barzun, Jacques, 106
Bassick High School (Connecticut), xi, 11
Battle of Cannae, 124
Bauer, Peter, 103
Baumgart, Alice, 205
Beautiful Losers (Francis), 150
Becker, Marvin, 186
Beethoven, Ludwig von, 166
Being and Time (Heidegger), 79
Being There (film), xiv–xv

Bell Curve, The (Herrnstein, Murray), xi–xii
Bendersky, Joseph, 79
Benjamin, Walter, 50
Bennett, William, 172
Benoist, Alain de, 58
Berman, Russell, 79, 80, 87, 91
Berns, Walter, 30
Bernstein, Leonard, 166
Bloom, Allan, 100–101
Bottai, Giovanni, 91
Bradford, Doug, 195
Bradford, M. E., 171, 173, 174, 192–97
Bradford, Marie, 195, 196
Brandeis University, 46, 51
Bread Loaf (Middlebury College), 172
Bridgeport, Connecticut, xi, 7, 10, 23, 49, 101
  fire department of, 1
  Hungarian Jewish community in, 13
Broder, David, 131
Brooklyn College, 101
Brown, David, 161
Bryce, James, 197
Buchanan, Angela "Bay," 128, 152
Buchanan, James, 33
Buchanan, Patrick J., 106, 123–32, 136, 144, 149, 152, 154, 157, 181

Israel and, 127
presidential campaign of, 156
Buchanan, Shelley, 126, 145
Buckley, William F. Jr., 69, 119, 126, 173, 174
Budapest 1900 (Lukacs), 105
Budapest, Hungary, 4, 10
Burke, Edmund, 32, 60, 172, 175, 194
Burnham, James, 74-75, 188
Bush, George H. W., 94, 123, 125
Bush, George W., 94, 157

C
Calvin, John, 102
Case Western Reserve University, 3, 28, 31, 64, 167, 178, 186
Castro, Fidel, 45
Cathey, Boyd, 169
Catholic Church, 127
Catholic Intellectuals and Conservative Politics in America (Allitt), 98
Catholic University of America, 33, 36, 117, 179, 197
Cato Institute, 153
"Celestial Railroad, The" (Hawthorne), vii
Chambers, Whittaker, 135
Cheney, Lynne, 172, 174
Chernowitz, Maurice, 24
Chernowitz, Rose, 25

Chestnut Hill College, xvii, 113, 116, 117
Chou En-lai, 140
Chronicles, 140, 158
Churchill, Winston, 106, 147
Civil Rights Act (1964), 119
Civil War, 38, 194
Clinton, Bill, 130
Clinton, Hillary, 43
"cognitive elite," xii
Cole, Wayne S., 109
Columbia University, 34, 143, 197
Commentary, 37, 38, 43, 106, 127, 129, 182
Communist Party, 189
author's father and, 7
Communists, 5, 6, 45, 47, 98, 110, 135, 140, 184, 186
Will Herberg and, 70
Conceived in Liberty (Rothbard), 154
Confederacy, 196
Confessions of an Original Sinner (Lukacs), 98
Congdon, Lee, 106
Congress of Vienna, 146
Conservatism in America (Gottfried), 35, 37
Conservatism (Nisbet), 199
Conservative Intellectual Movement in America, The (Nash), 69

Conservative Mind, The (Kirk), 156
Conservative Movement, The (Gottfried), 20, 105, 126
Cornell University, 11, 48
Counterrevolution, The (Molnar), 99
Criton (Plato), 60
Crowley, Monica, 143
Crutchfield, Sylvia, 158

D
Dachau, 101
Danger on the Right (Foster and Epstein), 100
Dante, 174
Davis, Angela, 46
Day, Dorothy, 181
Decter, Midge, 182
Demjanjuk, Ivan, 128
Democracy and Populism (Lukacs), 110
democratic capitalism, 121
Dennis, William, 26
Depression, Great, 162
Dialectic of Enlightenment (Adorno and Horkheimer), 53–54
Die Dialektik der Aufklarung (Adorno), 92
Diggins, John Patrick, 75
Disraeli, Benjamin, 139
Doctorow, E. L., 113

Dollfuss, Engelbert, 6
Doenecke, Justus, 109
Dostoyevsky, Fyodor, 74
Douglas, Helen Gahagan, 135
Douglas, Melvyn, xv
Downs, Anthony, 114
Drew University, 64, 69
Duel (Lukacs), 106
Dulles, John Foster, 108–109

E
Economic Theory of Democracy (Downs), 114
Einstein, Albert, 70
Eisenhower, Dwight, 108–109, 136
Eliade, Mircea, 111
Eliot and His Age (Kirk), 156, 166
Elizabethtown College, xiii, xvii, 33, 34, 144, 180
Ellul, Jacques, 100
England, 191
Enlightenment, 111, 193
Epstein, Benjamin, 100
Equal Rights Amendment (ERA), 48
Eros and Civilization (Marcuse), 46
Ethics of the Fathers, 72
Eugene of Savoy, 97
Europe
  secularism and, 99

INDEX

F
Faludi, Susan, 181
Farias, Victor, 82
fascism, 111
Feith, Douglas, 157
Fest, Joachim, 128
Fleming, Thomas, 140, 169
Foner, Eric, 172
Fordham University, 117
Foreign Affairs, 137
Foster, Arnold, 100
Foundations of the Frankfurt School of Social Research (Tar), 55
Fox-Genovese, Elizabeth, 172, 185
   Catholicism of, 190
Fox News, 143, 159
Foxman, Abraham, 127
Francis, Samuel, 58, 86, 87, 130, 131, 149, 150–59, 156, 158, 167
   immigration and, 157
Frankfurt School of Social Research, 47, 52, 53, 55, 56, 80, 92
Frankfurter Allgemeine Zeitung, 37
Freiheit oder Gleichheit (Kuehnelt-Leddihn), 117
French Revolution, 101, 120
Freud, Sigmund, 46, 53
Friedman, Murray, 67
From Rebellion to Revolution (Genovese), 188

Front National, 93
Front, The (film), 91
Frost, Robert, 173, 175
Frum, David, 31
Fukuyama, Francis, 88
Fulbright Scholarship, 192
Fuller, Lon, 134
Furet, François, 112

G
Genesis, 117, 177
Genovese, Eugene, 171, 173, 174, 178, 183–92, 193, 194, 204
George, Stefan, 50, 51
Gerson, Mark, 42
Gibson, Mel, 65
Gingrich, Newt, 168
Giuliani, Rudolph, 94
Goldberg, Arthur, 48
Goldberger, Sam, 10, 11, 14
Goldwater, Barry, 52, 100
Gorbachev, Mikhail, 137
Gordon, David, 57
Gottfried, Andrew, 1–17
   as fire commissioner, 3
Gottfried, Barbara, 19–20, 32, 135, 205
Gottfried, Dana, xvi, 1, 13, 15, 28, 29–33, 64, 131, 167
   death of, 31, 33–34, 142, 183
Gottfried, Dennis, 205
Gottfried, Dorothea, 5

Gottfried, Emil, 5
Gottfried, Jonathan, 20
Gottfried, Joseph, 20, 32, 205
Gottfried, Mary, 32, 34–36, 41, 79, 80, 81, 92, 104, 176, 205
Gottfried, Paul (author's grandfather), 5
Gottfried, Ruth, 8
Gottfried, Sara, 20
Gouldner, Alvin, 79
Gramsci, Antonio, 57, 58, 189
Graz, Austria, 4
Great Powers and Eastern Europe, The (Lukacs), 103, 110
Griffin, Franny, 159
Griswold v. Connecticut, 49
Guggenheim Fellowship, 103, 132, 175, 185
Gundolf, Friedrich, 50

H

Habermas, Jürgen, 39, 43, 102
Habsburg Empire, 42, 164
Haig, Alexander, 146–47
Hamilton, Alexander, 120, 154
Hannah and Her Sisters (film), 177
Hannibal, 124
Harper University, 185
Harvard University, xii
Hawthorne, Nathaniel, vii
Hegel, G. W. F., 42, 45, 52, 59, 60, 134, 170, 189, 202

Heidegger, Martin, 46, 79, 82, 83, 100
Hellenikes Grammes (Athens), 37
Henry, Patrick, 193
Herberg, Will, xii, 63–75, 159, 188
  dining habits of, 73
  Mafia and, 71
Herblock (Herbert L. Block), 134
Heritage Foundation, 82, 165, 170
Herrnstein, Richard, xi
Hertzog, Phares, 144
Hillsdale College, 103
Himmelfarb, Gertrude, 176, 200
Hiss, Alger, 135
Histoire Intellectuelle du Libéralisme (Manent), 58
Historical Consciousness (Lukacs), 103, 107
Historical Society, 190
Histories (Thucydides), 60
History of the Idea of Progress (Nisbet), 201
Hitler, Adolf, 3, 4, 6, 30, 83, 84, 101, 106, 109, 119
Hobbes, Thomas, 58, 134, 138
Hobsbawm, Eric, 184–85
Holborn, Hajo, 27–28
Holland, 191
Hollander, Robert, 173, 174
Holocaust, 3

Hook, Sidney, 52, 67, 106
Hoover, Herbert, 160
Horkheimer, Max, 52, 53–54
Horowitz, David, 25, 67, 68
Horowitz, Irving Louis, 200
Horthy, Miklos, 5, 11
Hume, David, xvi
Huntington, Samuel, xi
Hussein, Saddam, 94
Husserl, Edmund, 83, 92
Hyde Park, New York, 4, 10

I
immigration, 113, 157
In These Times (Postel), 82
Ingersoll Prize, 165, 198
Intercollegiate Studies Institute (ISI), 53, 63, 72, 103
Irrepressible Rothbard, The (Rockwell), 162
Ivanhoe (Scott), xi

J
Jablecki, Juliusz, 43
Jäger, Lorenz, 47
Jarrett, Beverly, xv
Jefferson Lecture in the Humanities, 156, 198
Jefferson, Thomas, 193
Jerusalem, 10
Jesuits, the
  see Society of Jesus

John, Gospel of, 117
John Randolph Club, 154
Johnson, Lyndon B., 25, 52
Johnson, Samuel, xvi
Judiciary Act of 1789, 58
Judis, John, 126
Julius Caesar, x

K
Kahler, Eric, 50
Kant, Immanuel, 45, 102, 163
Kaplan, Morton, 133
Kennan, George, 106, 138
Kennedy, Edward, 172
Kennedy, John F., 52, 68, 136
King, Martin Luther Jr., 38, 69, 136, 187
Kirk, Annette, 29, 149, 150, 167
Kirk, Monica, 29, 167–168
Kirk, Russell, 28–29, 149, 150, 152–53, 159, 165–70
  Buchanan campaign and, 156
  editorials in *National Review* and, 169
  insurance and, 155
Kirkwood, R. Cort, 2
Kissinger, Henry, 137, 145
Klein, Robert, 48
Kolko, Gabriel, 161
Koszinski, Jerzy, xiv
Kraditor, Aileen, 189
Krauthammer, Charles, 68

Kristol, Irving, 67, 162
Kronstadt uprising (1921), 74
Kuehnelt-Leddihn, Erik, 97–98, 101, 115–22
  monarchism and, 98
Kun, Bela, 5
Kurth, James, 23, 39, 138

L
"L'âme et la machine" (Molnar), 99
Lapham, Lewis, 106
Lasch, Christopher, 94, 171, 178–83
  Presbyterianism of, 181–82
Lasch-Quinn, Elisabeth, 182
Le modèle défiguré (Molnar), 98
Le socialisme sans visage (Molnar), 102
Leaders (Nixon), 139
"Leap Across the Sea, The" (Lukacs), 112
Ledeen, Michael, 42
Lee, Robert E., 2, 158
Left, 99, 109, 111, 118, 189
  Judeo-Christianity and the, 112
Leftism (Kuehnelt-Leddihn), 118–19
Lega Nord, 77, 93
Lenin, V. I., 74, 110
Likud Party, 38
Lincoln, Abraham, 136, 171, 194

Lind, Michael, 157
Locke, John, 162
Lopez, Roberto, 27
Luhr, Geret, 50
Lukacs, John, xvii, 97–98, 101, 103–15, 116, 121, 205
  anti-anticommunism and, 109–10
  neoconservatives and, 106
Luke, Tim, 80
Luther, Martin, 102, 118

M
Machiavelli, 58
Maistre, Joseph de, 46, 59, 60, 101
Manent, Pierre, 58–59
Mao Zedong, 136
Marcuse, Herbert, 25, 27, 45–61
Marsden, George, 28
Marshner, William, 26
Marx, Karl, 46, 49, 52, 53, 56, 80, 83, 172, 184, 187, 189, 201
McCarthy, Eugene, 169
McCarthy, Joseph, x, 26, 37, 64, 67, 91, 106, 141
  Will Herberg on, 68
McDonald, Forrest, 140, 194
McDonald, Wesley, 34, 53, 73, 168
Mecosta, Michigan, 29, 150, 165, 167

Medved, Michael, 130
Meinecke, Friedrich, 108
Metternich, Prince Klemens Wenzel von, 146
Meyer, Elsie, 27
Meyer, Eugene, 27
Meyer, Frank, 27
Michael, King, of Rumania, 191
Michigan State University, 28, 150, 195
Michnik, Adam, 43
Middlebury College, 172, 175
Mill, James, 155
Mind of the Master Class, The (Genovese and Fox-Genovese), 188
Mises, Ludwig von, 163
Modern Age, 38, 42
Molnar, Thomas, 23, 97–103, 122
   Catholic traditionalism and, 99
   Dachau and, 101
   Third World and, 102
Montesquieu, 58–59
More, Thomas, 26
Moscow, Russia, 6
Moses, 145
Mozart, Wolfgang, 56, 166
multiculturalism, xiii, 99, 184
Multiculturalism and the Politics of Guilt (Gottfried), 26, 35, 37
Murray, Charles, xi
Mussolini, Benito, 90, 110

N
NAS
   see National Association of Scholars
Nash, George, 69, 168
Nation, 158
National Association of Scholars (NAS), 190
National Endowment for the Humanities (NEH), 156, 171, 173, 175, 177, 192, 198
National Review, 27, 52, 68, 70, 72, 117, 135, 137, 146, 154, 170, 184, 197
   Kirk, Russell, and, 169
Nauert, Heather, 143
Nazis, 1, 6, 82, 93, 98, 109, 111, 119, 128, 129, 145, 158, 169
negative dialectic, 53
Negative Dialektik (Adorno), 92
NEH
   see National Endowment for the Humanities
Neoconservative Revolution, The (Friedman), 67
neoconservatism, 33, 36, 38, 40, 43, 53, 106, 126, 172, 174
New Deal, 155, 198
New History of the Cold War, A (Lukacs), 103, 108
New Left, 46, 178
New Oxford Review, 181

New Republic, 37, 41
New York Review of Books, 37, 181
New York Times, 43, 130, 136, 157, 181
New York University, xiii, 31, 64
  Law School of, 11
Nicomachean Ethics (Aristotle), 10
Niebuhr, Reinhold, 73
Niebuhr, Ursula, 73
Nietzsche, Friedrich, 83
Nisbet, Caroline, 115, 197, 198
Nisbet, Robert, 115, 133, 171, 197–204
  idea of progress and, 202
  leukemia of, 199
Nixon, Patricia, 142
Nixon, Richard, xvii, 31, 64, 124–25, 132–47, 178, 186, 200
  affirmative action and, 135
  as mixologist, 141–42
  Quakerism of, 141
  "skull sessions" and, 139
"Nixon Visited and Revisited" (Gottfried), 135
Nolte, Ernst, 111–12
Northern Illinois University Press, 132
Novak, James, 80
Novak, Michael, 80, 99
Novak, Naomi, 80, 92

O
O'Connor, Kathy, 133
Orbis, 39
Ost, David, 80, 88
Outgrowing Democracy (Lukacs), 112, 114

P
Paine, Thomas, 155
paleoconservatism, 160
paleolibertarianism, 160
Pan, David, 79, 80
Panunzio, Nick, 2, 15
Pareto, Vilfredo, 105
Paris, 10
  uprising of 1848, 49
Party of the Right (Yale), 27, 45
Pascal, Blaise, 46
Passing of the Modern Age, The (Lukacs), 103
Peale, Norman Vincent, 144
Pearson, Drew, 141
Peddie School, 144, 145
Pellicani, Luciano, 88
Philadelphia 1900–1950 (Lukacs), 112
Philadelphia Inquirer, 145
Philadelphia, Penn., 10, 26
Philadelphia Plan (1969), 135
Philadelphia Society, 192
Phillips, Kevin, 125
Philosophy of Right (Hegel), 59

Piano, The, (film) 162–63
Piccone, Mary, 77–78
Piccone, Paul, 53, 55, 77–95
Pickford, Mary, 12
Pittorelli, Eve, 48
Plato, 60, 154
Podhoretz, Norman, 42, 68, 174, 196
Pol Pot, 119
Poland, 1, 31, 43, 127
Policy Review, 199
Political Religions (Voegelin), 60
Polybius, 42
Postel, Danny, 82, 83, 84, 87
    on Paul Piccone, 85
Present Age, The (Nisbet), 200, 201
Princeton University, 174
Princeton University Press, 41
Protestant, Catholic, Jew (Herberg), 65
Proudhon, Paul, 46
Proust, Emile, 24
Puritans, 175

Q
Quakerism, 141
Quest for Community, The (Nisbet), 200–203

R
Radosh, Ronald, 68
Ragtime (Doctorow), 113
Raimondo, Justin, 163
Ramadan, 187
Rand, Ayn, 73
Reactionary Imperative, The (Bradford), 193
Reagan, Nancy, 143
Reagan, Ronald, 48, 137, 143, 156, 172, 174, 192, 204
Real Men (Kirkwood), 2
Reason and Revelation (Marcuse), 52
Reed, John Shelton, 191
Reflections on the Revolution in France (Burke), 60
Religious Right, 199
"Religious 'Right' to Violate the Law, A" (Herberg), 68
Republican National Convention, 130
Revolt of the Elites (Lasch), 181, 182
Rhetoric (Aristotle), 194
Richard Nixon Library, 133, 143
Right from the Beginning (Buchanan), 125, 126
Rittersporn, Gabor, 80
Rockford College, xiii, 27, 31, 48, 63, 100, 109, 143, 171, 173, 175, 179
Rockford, Illinois, ix, 15–16
Rockford Institute, 160, 198

Rockwell, Lew, 162
Roosevelt, Franklin D., 4, 136, 160, 198
Roosevelt University, 178
Rorty, Richard, 102
Rosen, Stanley, 46
Rosenthal, Abe, 127
Roth, Jack J., 178
Rothbard, Joey, 160
Rothbard, Murray, 129, 149, 152, 155, 159, 160–165, 167, 170, 174
Rousseau, Jean-Jacques, 58–59, 175
Rutgers University, 186
Ryn, Claes, 117, 132, 140, 143, 180

S
Saint Peter's College, 117
Salmagundi, 113
Santayana, George, 73
Schadler, Robert, 72
Schiller, Friedrich, 166
Schlesinger, Arthur, 161
Schmitt, Carl, 23, 53, 56, 84, 88, 90, 105
Schopenhauer, Arthur, 24, 46
Schwab, George, 55, 140
Schweitzer, Albert, 197
scientism, 107
Scott, Hugh, 26

Scott, Sir Walter, xi
Scottish Enlightenment, 163
Search for Historical Meaning, The (Gottfried), viii, 65, 103, 132, 197
Second Punic War, 124
Seize the Moment (Nixon), 139
Senate, U.S., 141
Six Days War, 25
Smith, Adam, 163
Society, 67
Society of Jesus, 163
Sociological Tradition, The (Nisbet), 202
Sociology as an Art Form (Nisbet), 201
Socrates, 159
Soirées (Maistre), 59
Sorel, Georges, 150
Southern Agrarians, 190, 192
Southern Tradition, The (Genovese), 188
Soviet Union, 1, 110, 119, 133, 154, 177, 178
Spencer, Richard, 206
Spinoza, Baruch, 22, 24
Stalin, Josef, 3, 4, 43, 109, 177, 179
Stampp, Kenneth, 189
Stanlis, Eleanor, 175
Stanlis, Peter, 32, 63, 156, 171, 174–77, 192

State of Emergency (Buchanan), 130, 157
Stern des Bundes (George), 51
Stone, Brad Lowell, 199
Strange Death of Marxism, The (Gottfried), 37
Strasburg, Pennsylvania, vii–viii, xvii, 19
Strauss, Leo, 83, 194
Supreme Court, 115
Sydow, Max von, 177

T
Taft, Robert, xiii, 170
Tar, Zoltan, 55
Taylor, John, 143
Taylor, John (of Caroline), 193
Teggart, Frederick, 201
Telos, 53, 54–55, 57, 77, 79, 80, 81, 82, 84, 85, 89, 186
The World and I, 32–33, 85, 116, 126, 133, 158, 196
 Kirk, Russell, and, 165
Theodoracopulos, "Taki," 13, 38, 206
Theory of History (Teggart), 202
Thomas, Corey, xiii–xiv
Thomas, Norman, 168
Thread of Years, A (Lukacs), 112
Thucydides, 60
Tonsor, Stephen, 185
Transaction Press, 200

Treaty of Versailles, 109
Triple R, 162
True and Only Heaven, The (Lasch), 180, 182
Truman, Harry, 106, 136–137
Twin Powers (Molnar), 99

U
Ukraine, 128
Ulmen, Gary, 55, 80, 81–82, 84, 86, 88
University of Budapest, 98
University of California, Berkeley, xii, 189
University of California, Los Angeles, 105
University of Dallas, 171, 196
University of Michigan, 185
University of Missouri Press, xv
University of Nevada, 160
University of North Carolina, 190–91
University of Rochester, 172, 178, 185, 191
University of Wisconsin, 161
Up From Communism (Diggins), 75

V
Van Kley, Dale, 27
Verlag, Leopold Stocker, 4
Vienna, Austria, 5, 10

Vivaldi, Antonio, 56
Voegelin, Eric, 60

W
Wall Street Journal, 66, 130
Wallace, George, 195
Warren, Donald, 156
Washington, George, 2
Washington Post, 130, 136, 157, 173
Washington Times, 33, 130, 131, 157
Washington University (St. Louis), 79
WASPs, xiv, 26, 114, 164
Watergate, 125, 134
Weaver, Richard M., 194
Weber, Max, 88, 164
Weekly Standard, 159
Wesner, Gordon, 27
Who's Who in the World, viii
Wiggershaus, Rolf, 54
Wilhelm, Kaiser, 160
Will, George, 68, 106
William of Ockham, 102
Williams, William Appleman, 161
Wills, Garry, 140
Wilson, Woodrow, 36, 49, 109, 136–37, 138, 155, 162
Wittfogel, Karl, 55
Wohl, Robert, 105
Wolfe, Alan, 41
Wolin, Richard, 84
World Restored, A (Kissinger), 145–46
World the Slaveholders Made, The (Genovese), 188
World War I, 5, 13, 34, 38, 66, 108, 109, 160
World War II, 54, 109, 169, 198, 200
Worthy Company, A (Bradford), 193

Y
Yale University, 11, 25, 45, 49, 51
Yeshiva University, 11, 21, 24, 47

Z
Zavlasky, Victor, 80

About the Author

Paul E. Gottfried is Professor of Humanities and holds the Raffensperger Chair in the Department of Political Science at Elizabethtown College. A distinguished historian and interpreter of the American conservative movement, he is the author of numerous books, including *Conservatism in America: Making Sense of the American Right*, *Multiculturalism and the Politics of Guilt: Towards a Secular Theocracy*, and *After Liberalism: Mass Democracy in the Managerial State*.